KEEPING IT LOCAL

CHANGE AND DEVELOPMENT IN AN
INDIAN TRIBAL COMMUNITY

KEEPING IT LOCAL

CHANGE AND DEVELOPMENT IN AN INDIAN TRIBAL COMMUNITY

Pamela MacKenzie

A P H PUBLISHING CORPORATION
5 ANSARI ROAD, DARYA GANJ
NEW DELHI-110 002

Published by
S.B. Nangia
A P H Publishing Corporation
5 Ansari Road, Darya Ganj
New Delhi-110002
☎ 23274050
Email : aphbooks@vsnl.net

ISBN 81-313-0131-1

2006

Typesetting at
Paragon Computers
B-36, Chanakya Place
New Delhi-110 059
☎ 25509417

Printed at
Balaji offset
Navin Shahdara,Delhi-32
Ph:22324437

CONTENTS

FOREWORD

Occasionally, when involved in international development, one encounters projects which are so memorable that, whatever their problems or shortcomings, they stand out as models of what development activities can be. Such is the project described in this book, which sets forth the long, complex journey by which the impoverished and marginalized tribal Adiwasi-Oriya language people of the Araku Valley, Andhra Pradesh, India, have moved step by step towards the modern globalised world.

As a consultant for the Canadian International Development Agency (CIDA), my experience with the program began with an evaluation visit in the mid-1980s and was followed by similar visits until the year 2000. My host on these occasions was the Canadian linguist Uwe Gustafsson who, with his wife Elke, had been living in the tribal village of Hattaguda since 1970, forming a close relationship with the local people and a deep understanding of their values and culture. The Gustafssons' steadfast commitment to improving the lives of the people- a commitment which still persists- was remarkable, as was Uwe's dedicated linguistic research and later role as Project Co-ordinator. By 1984 this had led, among other achievements, to the development of a written language for the Adiwasi-Oriya speaking people, together with large-scale literacy programming and village adult education initiatives. These were to be followed by the 1988 establishment of the tribal NGO AASSAV, with responsibility for management and leadership of the income generating project phase, and for the negotiations and arrangements which became necessary with government and non-government agencies and organizations.

In some 30 years of international experience, in which I had seen well over one hundred literacy, education and development projects in Africa, Asia and Latin America, I felt from my first visit, confirmed in my later evaluation missions, that the AASSAV project was one of the most extraordinary I had encountered. Despite differences in scale and resources, it reminded me of MOBRAL, the national literacy and development program of the Brazilian government in the 1970s and early 1980s, which I had visited as Director of UNESCO's Experimental World Literacy Program (EWLP). In both cases literacy was seen, not as an end in itself, but as a first step on the road to self-sufficiency and an improved quality of life. Both programs were also noteworthy for their high standards of planning, administration, and conscientious and detailed record keeping. In the AASSAV program the income generating component was based on a variety of agricultural and animal husbandry initiatives, while in MOBRAL, employment agencies, factories, technical institutes, shops and industries were associated directly with literacy centres to facilitate employment and further training as required.

In its linkage with literacy and its efforts with income generating activities, the AASSAV program also had certain elements in common with UNESCO's functional literacy approach, which emphasized the highly practical ways in which literacy could transform people's lives. In the EWLP program of UNESCO, however, the functional element was largely confined to, and formed a major portion of, the literacy curriculum, while the AASSAV and MOBRAL approach incorporated a wider variety of post-literacy options.

What else did I find so remarkable in the AASSAV project? Firstly, the close relationship between Uwe Gustafsson, as an expatriate, and the local population. From the early stages of linguistic research, the project was inclusive of the needs and culture of the local people. Such an approach, unfortunately ignored by too many development agencies, is an important element if local commitment and sustainability are to be achieved. By 1988, project management was almost entirely assumed by the members of AASSAV, with Uwe Gustafsson wisely stepping back but continuing to provide guidance and support in an advisory capacity.

A second noteworthy element has been the project's unusually long time-frame. Development projects normally receive external support for four or five years, occasionally followed by short extensions. In this context, the necessary training, capacity building and long term vision required for sustainability can seldom be achieved. The AASSAV program has avoided this in two ways: by the leadership, support and continuity provided by Uwe and Elke Gustafsson in one capacity or another since 1970, and by the unusually long term funding from CIDA which, despite delays and obstacles, covered much of the period between 1983 and 2000. This has provided opportunity for training and learning by AASSAV members as they faced the many problems associated with income generating activities and negotiations with government departments and NGOs.

These problems have been serious. Few of the income generating projects have been fully successful, while negotiations with government agencies and NGOs for linkages, partnerships and support have frequently been frustrated by bureaucratic delays and evasions. From this however AASSAV has clearly gained valuable experience for the future.

The overall project raises interesting questions that are relevant to our contemporary world.

To what extent can (or should) tribal communities integrate with globalised societies? To what extent does this require loss or transformation of traditional cultures? Is this desirable, inevitable, or can a balance be achieved?

To what extent does long term sustainability depend on local input, ideas and participation in every aspect of development planning and programming?

To what extent are governments and NGOs willing to abandon short project time-frames and develop the long term plans with their local partners which we now realise sustainable social and economic improvements inevitably require.

Finally, we might well ask whether it is realistic to expect tribal or community groups or NGOs, working to bring sustainable economies to impoverished areas of developing countries, to attain internal self-sufficiency during their struggle, something which few of the large scale established national and international NGOs themselves are able to achieve.

This book, with its well written, comprehensive, objective analyses, is a tribute to the remarkable efforts by which a tribal society, with support from dedicated and committed expatriates, has progressed towards a better life, despite disappointments and still unresolved problems. Of over 100,000 mother tongue speakers of Adiwasi-Oriya in a 50 kilometre by 100 kilometre area of Andhra Pradesh, over 11,000 have achieved literacy in their mother tongue, and including a large number in Telugu, the official state language. The program in its many dimensions has thus benefited a large percentage of the Adiwasi-Oriya speaking families of Andhra Pradesh. The establishment of AASSAV, and the experience, the learning and confidence acquired by its members, opens the way for further advance. For a previously marginalized tribal society, impoverished and without a written language a generation ago, these and other achievements are impressive.

John C. Cairns,
Elora, Ontario, Canada

ACKNOWLEDGEMENTS

It has been a privilege to have been able to research a book such as this one. The research has given me an opportunity to walk for a short time with a group of people who have had to struggle to make their way in a changing world; a particularly difficult challenge for a people who have until recent years lived in isolation, at the margins of the modern world.

I would like to thank all the members of AASSAV, and the communities they serve, who so kindly and graciously allowed me access to their lives and their efforts and the daily challenges. Each visit to AASSAV and the communities they serve was pleasant, enjoyable and positive.

I would particularly like to extend my thanks to the President of AASSAV, Mr Raghunadh and to the Vice President, Mr Arjun who acted as my translator. I would also like to thank all those who granted interviews, from the Executive Committee and members of AASSAV, and to all the recipients of the work of AASSAV.

I would like to acknowledge the help given to me by those working in the government agencies – the Integrated Tribal Development Agency (ITDA), and the District Rural Development Agency (DRDA) – and to the Non Governmental Agencies (NGOs) with which AASSAV is connected; in particular, CARE India and Naandi, all of whom offered valuable insights.

Without the coordinator's help, Mr Uwe Gustafsson and his organisation, LEAD in Canada, the book would not have been written and it is thanks to them that all of this was possible.

I would like to acknowledge the guidance of Dr Clinton Robinson whose idea it was to write the book, and thank him for his support; and to Professor John Cairns for his willingness to write foreword, and whose positive attitude to AASSAV over the years yielded much. Finally, many thanks to my sister, Mary Wheeler, who spent hours checking and rechecking, and asking pertinent questions.

It was a great honour to have been able to write this book and I dedicate it to all who struggle for life in the tribal regions and to those who struggle with them.

Pamela Mackenzie, 2006

ACRONYMS

AASSAV	Adivasi Abhivruddi Samskruthika Sangam, Araku Valley (*The Tribal Development and Cultural Society, Araku Valley*)
AOL	Action Oriented Learning
BICS	Basic interpersonal communicative skills
CALPS	Cognitive academic language proficiency
CAG	Community Action Groups
CBO	Community Based Organisation
CC	Community Coordinator
CIDA	Canadian International Development Agency
DC	District Collector
DRDA	District Rural Development Agency
EC	Executive Committee
IGA	Income Generating Activities
INGO	International Non Governmental Organisation
ITDA	Integrated Tribal Development Agency
MLP	Micro Level Planning
MPDO	Mandal P
NGO	Non Governmental Organisation
ODI	Overseas Development Institute, London
PO	Project Officer
PRA	Participatory Rural Appraisal
SGH	Self Help Groups

Coffee Plantations: Dumbriguda 1988

Coffee Plantations: Dumbriguda 2000

Coffee Plantations: Dumbriguda first banana plantation 1988

Coffee Plantations: Dumbriguda potato field 1991

Coffee Plantations: Dumbriguda silver oak in 1993

Coffee Plantations: Ravvalguda Plantation 2004

Coffee Plantations: Working on the plantation

Coffee Plantations: Young coffee saplings in AASSAV nursery

Headquaters office now

Headquaters office as new

Literacy class in 2003

AASSAV dairy farm

CARE STEP spring water supply

Tribal woman learning to read and write in 2003

Women's Self Help Group Meeting

Elke takes Zogubandu to hospital

Introduction

The early morning sun rises through the veils of mist lying low over the valley and the surrounding hillsides. Smoke begins to seep through the grass roofs of mud built homes where the women are busy with the first chores of the morning. Some are cooking ragi, the nutritious porridge their family will eat to start the day. Others are sweeping the compound with brooms made from forest grass. Still others are carrying cow dung in baskets on their heads along the dusty road. They are taking it to the fields to be used later as fertilizer. Children begin to stir, wrapped in warm cloths against the chill air, ready, after completing their chores, to attend the single classroom, multigrade government school. Parents face another day of work to provide sufficient for their families. Women will plant, harvest, go to the market with saleable goods, collect wood and water, cook and clean, while men will plough, weed or attend the market.

In many ways the life of this tribal community in the eastern Indian state of Andhra Pradesh appears to have changed little over the centuries. But for this once remote mountain region change is inevitable as it becomes increasingly subject to outside influence, traditional sources of livelihoods cease to exist and old ways of life cannot be maintained. How that change is managed depends on the capacity of the communities to recognize what is happening and make informed choices about the future; informed, that is, by a sufficient awareness of the consequences of those choices. In practice however this is a process which usually occurs without adequate preparation or understanding, so there is confusion, anxiety and tension as they make their inevitable adjustments to the impact of changes beyond their control.

This book tells the story of how one Indian tribal community struggled with poverty, marginalisation and change, learning to become self-reliant and self-confident in organising and managing their own development. On the face of it, this is an unlikely story, one of success and failure, of empowerment and frustration, the story of a long road patiently trodden. It bears the hallmarks of much development practice anywhere in the world, but it is

distinctive in its particular circumstances and especially in the
marked social exclusion of the community from the wider society.

The research for this book spanned three years; the author visited
the region several times at different seasons from 2001 to 2004,
staying at the headquarters of the *Adivasi Abhivrudi Samskruthika
Sangam Araku Valley*, literally the Tribal Community
Development Society, Araku Valley, or *AASSAV*, as the tribal
NGO is known. During these visits she interviewed members and
ex-members, staff at headquarters, the coordinator, those who had
gone through literacy training, those who had gone through
government training conducted by AASSAV, coffee farmers and
local villagers. She also talked with government officials in Araku
Valley, Paderu (the Agency headquarters), Visakhapatnam (the
District headquarters) and in Hyderabad (the State headquarters)
who had been involved with AASSAV in various capacities and
projects. She visited the Secretary of Tribal Welfare, officers at
the Tribal Welfare offices in Hyderabad and the Project Director
of the Integrated Tribal Development Agency, the government
agency which looks after development in the agency area.

The author also accompanied the president of AASSAV, the Vice
President and supervisors on village visits and attended meetings
of the Executive Committee; she sat in on training for supervisors,
meetings with coffee farmers, AASSAV members and staff of the
local bank, attended meetings with government officials and
observed the general running of the headquarters. Written material
that had been produced by AASSAV, such as reports,
correspondence, and incidental articles produced for donors and
other interested groups, were collected and analysed.

The vice-president of AASSAV, Arjun, who had attended an
English medium school, acted as translator and accompanied the
author on all her visits, except those in Hyderabad. The vice-
president's sister, who also spoke some English, sometimes joined
them, particularly where it was specifically known that women
would be the focus of interviews. With the help of the expatriate
coordinator, Uwe Gustafsson from Canada, the author was able to
view the whole work from many perspectives.

Research in such complex and remote situations cannot be done
systematically by appointment or pre-planning; opportunities had
to be taken when they arose. There were constant logistical
obstacles, so the development of an adequate understanding and
knowledge of the situation demanded time and patience. The

difficulties experienced by the author are in themselves an indication of why any development that has occurred in this region has been a struggle.

Themes of the book

While this book is not intended to be academic in tone or style, the story of AASSAV raises important development issues common to many communities, NGOs and donors across the world.

Chapter 1 is an introduction to the socio-economic, cultural and political aspects of the tribal communities of this region. Various themes and issues are then explored through the experiences of AASSAV including the links between literacy and development, local participation and capacity building, women's participation, donor and partner relationships including the role of an expatriate coordinator, and sustainability.

Chapter 2 looks at the literacy programme which formed the foundation of the later development work. It looks at what languages were used in literacy and why they were selected and at the pedagogical and educational methods that were used in the literacy programme in relation to the design and production of materials as well as in classroom practice. It looks at the delivery system used in terms of organisation, supervision, assessment and evaluation. It also discusses the gender balance in the literacy programme with regard to learners, instructors, supervisors, trainers and managers. Since female participation in the literacy programme has been relatively low, the reasons for this are explored and compared with parallel or contrasting experiences elsewhere in India. Finally, it looks at the relationship between literacy and development in the local context.

Chapter 3 focuses on the institutional development of AASSAV. It traces the historical development of the NGO in its context and how it developed into this particular form of NGO. It includes how its partnerships with government, donors, other NGOs and with the community have shaped its growth, including the choice of projects and other development activities. Attempts are made to explain the surprises that came up along the way and unresolved issues are set out with as much clarity as possible.

Chapter 4 explores the organisation and management of AASSAV. It looks at who has participated in the project and how participation has evolved for employees, trainees, associated

farmers, outside onlookers and planners. It explains some of the
social and other barriers to participation and the prospects for
expanding the range of participants. The role and changing
contribution of Uwe Gustafsson, an expatriate, is described and
discussed with reference to the literature on external change
agents. The long-term nature of an expatriate's input is debated to
elucidate the different phases there have been in the nature of that
input and to assess its impact.

Chapter 5 explores AASSAV's connections with its partners
showing both positive and negative outcomes of these various
relationships with government, donors and with other NGO
development agencies. It explores the type of support provided,
such as capacity building, and the struggles it has experienced to
maintain local control.

Chapter 6 explores the issues of sustainability examined under
three areas which are discussed throughout the book: technical,
financial and managerial.

- *technical sustainability:* skills required as the programme
  developed in agriculture, carpentry, literacy, teaching and the
  supervision of teaching, chicken rearing, water management
  and so on. How these skills were acquired and how firmly
  they were embedded in the project personnel.
- *financial sustainability:* the financial growth of the
  programme is sketched here with an indication of the
  necessary inputs and how they are related to achieving self-
  sustainability in the financial area. The project contains a high
  number of income-generating aspects and their successes,
  failures and current potential are described and explained.
  Summary charts of the financial inputs and outputs are
  included.
- *managerial sustainability:* explores how the project developed
  leadership and management skills, how people were selected
  for these roles and how they carried them out, the kind of
  management structure which evolved and how this sits with
  local cultural patterns of management and leadership. For
  example, are decisions made and decision-making processes
  patterned after local existing practice? The influence of
  people in the community or outside the project who have or
  have had significant influence on the running of the project is
  explored.

The main points are summarized against the challenges and

difficulties as it seeks to understand the lessons which can be learned and the questions which continue to be asked in similar situations.

In conclusion, the impact of AASSAV in the community is considered, with particular attention paid to questions of empowerment; growing self-confidence, the increasing voice of this marginalised community with regard to government institutions and with regard to the changing links and relationships with non-tribal communities in the area. The perceptions of a wide range of different people in AASSAV and in the community towards economic aspects, growth of the cash economy, attitudes to education and school enrolment, the position of women and relations with mainstream society are considered.

The Epilogue provides a picture of the on going situation in April 2006 as AASSAV continues to work for its own and the community's development.

Each chapter is followed by a series of questions which can be used for discussion - a stimulus for further reflection on the development issues raised in it. This book gives an in-depth presentation and analysis of a significant and unusual development initiative, in the context of one of India's most marginalised social groups, a tribal community. As such it offers data, principles, warnings and ideas about development for marginalised groups elsewhere. The topics for discussion will serve to carry that larger debate forward.

CHAPTER 1

Araku Valley: The Culture, the People and the Land

Araku Valley[1] is a beautiful region in the mountains of the Paderu Agency of Visakhapatnam District in the State of Andhra Pradesh (AP) which is in the eastern central region of India. This District lies in the northern part of Andhra Pradesh, bordering on the State of Orissa. Five kilometres from the township of Araku Valley lies Hattaguda and it is here that AASSAV, the indigenous tribal development organisation, is located. The people of this region have been described by CARE India as marginalised and *"among the poorest and most deprived in India"*, and their situation as *"the most disadvantaged ... in terms of ... access to information, resources and opportunities, critical for their livelihood."* They live on *"dwindling minor forest produce"*, are exploited *"by unscrupulous traders from mainstream societies"* and *"land alienation by non-tribals"* is common *"despite protective legislation"*. Female literacy levels are very low (below 10%) with school dropout rates of 70% (1991 census) and *"Infant Mortality Rates of 212 per 1000 births, three times the State average."* Sustainable Tribal Empowerment Programme (STEP 2001)

It is the tribal communities of this region that this book is about. This chapter describes their language, culture and environment, and the circumstances in which they live.

Language and Culture

Many tribal groups live in the Paderu Agency on the border areas of Northern Andhra Pradesh and Orissa. There are about ten languages spoken among them. Out of these, four languages are predominantly spoken on the Andhra Pradesh side of the border: Adivasi Oriya, Kui Kond, Konda and Kupia. A few people speak the other languages although they have nearly died out in AP.

Adivasi Oriya is the mother tongue of the Kotia and Bagata tribal

---

[1] Araku Valley is both a region and the main town of the region.

communities and is the *lingua franca* for all the tribal communities in the area. It has become the first language of a number of other groups including the Konda Dora, and Valmikis, although the Konda Dora retain their language where they are the majority, usually in the more remote villages.

There are over 100,000 mother tongue speakers of Adivasi Oriya living in Andhra Pradesh in an area of about 50km by 100km. In Orissa another 120,000 or so people speak effectively the same language which they call Desia and which has 95% similarity Adivisi Oriya. Adivasi Oriya is a language of the Indo-Aryan family, related to Oriya, the official language of the neighbouring state of Orissa, but the standard Oriya, as taught in schools in Orissa, and Adivasi Oriya are not mutually intelligible.

In Andhra Pradesh, the official state language is Telugu, one of the Dravidian family of languages. All schooling and official communication takes place in Telugu and because the two languages belong to different language families it is difficult for Adivasi Oriya speakers to understand and learn the official language. Those who know Telugu use it to communicate with officers of the government, in some market transactions and with Telugu people they meet. Many women, particularly in isolated villages, do not speak or understand much Telugu. Children when they first attend school usually have no understanding of Telugu and if the teacher does not understand the tribal language, the difficulties for children are overwhelming and the dropout rate is high.

Social Order

Although the caste system was not originally part of tribal culture, recognition of caste has developed. The Bagatas and Kotias are the higher groups, then the Konda Doras and finally the Valmikis. The Valmikis, who settled in this region many generations ago, are good traders. Some from the smith caste also settled here. Neither were originally tribal, but now both groups have tribal status. The tribal groups generally intermingle, often living in the same village. Some villages are multilingual, while others are inhabited by single language groups. The class or caste composition of a village plays a significant role in determining behavioural patterns and perceptions.

Work

The Kotia, Bagata and Rana clans are traditionally agriculturalists and the life of these tribal people has for generations revolved around the seasons. Their main crop is rice, production of which has improved in recent years as a result of the introduction of new varieties and better irrigation, bringing more fields under cultivation. Several varieties of millet are also grown on "dry" fields where farmers depend on monsoon rains. Ragi, a highly nutritious millet from which the tribal people make porridge morning and evening, can also be grown on dry fields after the monsoon. Rapeseed, a cash crop, is planted after the millet. Various vegetables, pulses and fruits are also cultivated, mostly to be sold in the weekly market; the farmers keep hardly any to eat themselves. For example, as the price of lentils in the market is good they sell almost the entire crop. This supplements the income of the tribal farmer, but does not encourage good health. The government has also been encouraging the cultivation of vegetables and pulses to provide for the growing city of Visakhapatnam. Some tribal farmers now have coffee plantations on their waste or semi-waste hilly land developed with the help of the Coffee Board of India, ITDA, AASSAV and Naandi (See Chapter 3: Coffee Farmers Project).

There are various forest crops, each of which used to initiate a festival when there would be dancing and revelry, often all through the night. The gurus would pronounce when the season began, when the festivals would start, when they could eat the fruit and when the season ended.

The Valmikis are mainly traders and, although they speak a dialect of Adivasi Oriya, they are also competent speakers of Telugu. The Kui Kond and Konda speakers are involved in some agriculture, but still rely somewhat on the ever-diminishing jungle. In order to supplement their limited income through vegetables or forest products, many, both men and women, will hire themselves out as daily labourers. For people from the interior villages, however, opportunities to work as daily labourers are limited. They therefore often have to migrate to find work.

Division of Work

In subsistence situations, although it is essential that all work together for survival, women are often the hardest workers and are the most productive whether in land-based or non land-based circumstances; but they lose out to men when it comes to accessing the resources available and in decision-making power. The patriarchal structures of most societies and the subordination of women means that women's contributions are often ignored, repressed or undermined. Male perspectives dominate, causing women to yield to male authority and control.

Within the tribal communities both men and women have to work hard, but the greater burden of work falls on the women while the men are the decision makers. The Adivasi women get up before 5am and, depending on whether the village has electricity or not, will go to bed between 8-9pm. Women fetch water and cut and carry the wood; they cook the food, having prepared the ragi or rice beforehand by pounding it; they clean the house and look after the children. They look after the animal barns, cleaning the barns and taking the manure to the fields. They even do most of the heavy work: they plant, weed and harvest in the fields. Although the men also work in the fields, helping to weed, and thresh and winnow after harvesting, it is mainly women's work. The women inform the men of what needs to be supplied and it is the man's job to buy what is necessary. The women, however, accompany the men to market in order to help carry the heavy loads to market and back home.

There is little value in a person who cannot work hard and older people's work is not seen as a valuable contribution even though they are occupied in caring for small children when parents are working so that birds of prey will not take them, drying grains in the sun, sorting vegetables and feeding the animals. When the oldest son marries he takes over the running of the house, and the parents have to move out. No provision is made for old age and, as there is very little room in the house itself, the older people often have nowhere to go except onto the veranda. This can be rather uncomfortable in winter as temperatures drop. At times of sickness the older people have to go to the shelter made for the animals.

The Environment

The area of the Paderu Agency begins in the foothills of the eastern hill range (the Eastern Ghats) in the southeast and continues to the Orissa border in the northwest. The foothills start at a distance of about 60 to 70 kms from the coast of the Bay of Bengal. These hills rise to over 5000ft (1500m), most of the inhabited land lying around 3000ft (910m). The Agency is characterized by hilly terrain; flat arable land is scarce. Several rivers and streams run through the hills, most of which have water throughout the year, although since deforestation water is becoming scarcer during the hot season. This water is used for irrigation as well as for hydroelectric power projects.

The climate of the area is controlled by the prevailing winds from the Indian Ocean, which bring the monsoon rains from the southwest in mid-June. Precipitation is heavy from mid-June to mid-August. In September the winds reverse, coming from the northeast. Cyclonic storms over the Bay of Bengal are common from September to

November, often bringing an abundance of rain. December until June constitutes the dry season. The climate is cooler in December and January with temperatures from 10-15C. From February the temperatures rise to 30C in May and June. Rain, showers and thunderstorms are common from April onwards until the monsoon breaks in June.

Before the twentieth century, the entire area was a tropical wet forest, but today only remnants of such forests remain in precipitous gullies too narrow to farm and in the more interior mountain region. According to residents, even two generations ago there was widespread tropical forest throughout the entire area. Then, they say, rain was more regular, particularly between March and the monsoon season, and there was always running water, even in the hot season. Today any land that is not too steep or rocky to farm is under cultivation. The eroding soils yield less and less each year and the harvests are meagre in economic terms. Except for the rare gallery forests, what trees remain are either fruit trees or those planted for their economic value. Examination of the slopes above the valleys reveals a thin layer of humus - about 10 – 20cm - lying directly on the bedrock with no significant subsoil. The bedrock, mostly smooth-surface basalt, is consistent throughout a wide geographic area. At the foot of the slopes there is evidence of considerable slumping of soils from above, often in the form of landslides. This topography and climate have constrained and influenced the agricultural practices followed today.

The residents of the area identify three types of soil: black, red and sand. The black soils, which lie on the first terrace above the streams in the valley floor, contain humus, some of it remaining from the previous forest environment, and some of it carried down from the eroding hillsides. These rich, loose soils are used for wet rice cultivation. The red soils are found on the steep deforested hillsides and at the base of those hills. They are planted with rapeseed and millet in dry land farming. The sandy soils, which lie mostly in the zone between the red and the black soils, are used primarily for growing certain root and vegetable crops like potatoes, tomatoes, eggplant, and cabbage.

The need for arable land, for firewood, and for housing material has denuded the hillsides of most of the trees. Much of the forest has been destroyed in the last 20-30 years when trees were cut down and taken out by night. The authorities argued that the lawlessness in the region made it too hard for them to control the destruction. The vegetation in uncultivated areas is mostly secondary growth; shrubs and weeds unpalatable to cattle, goats, sheep and buffalo that forage the hillsides. Because grazing is intense, grass has little opportunity to get established, increasing the erosion problem created by clearing the forest.

Podu (shifting cultivation) is still practised by some of the tribals and a plot once cleared is quickly robbed of fertility by soil erosion. It is abandoned after two or three years of cultivation, but with an adverse, cumulative impact on the environment. In the constant search for firewood, every month an estimated 5,000 tons of wood is carried in head loads to meet the fuel needs of the tribal belt.

The environment in the Agency can be described as degraded, to the point of constituting an imminent danger to the survival of the local population and it is only during recent years that the government has realised the seriousness of the situation. If the degradation continues, the people of this region will soon have no livelihoods and will be in need of state handouts. The government, it is true, is already working on various schemes to reverse this trend through coffee plantation, sericulture and social forestry plantations. Government forestland has been opened up for reforestation and the tribal people are given the right to work on reserved land through a paper of registration, which legally shares the ownership of the land between the tribal community and the government. But a more sharply focussed awareness of the root environmental issues that have produced the problems and the active participation of the local people in their solution are needed if the response is to be commensurate with the depth and urgency of the impending human disaster.

In sum then, the tribal population suffers because of the lack of an adequate economic base, which has been and still is deteriorating as a result of deforestation, climatic changes and the damaging agricultural methods practised. But attempts to help often falter; the barriers of language and culture and the tribal suspicion of outsiders hinder positive communication so that it is difficult to break the cycles of distrust and dislike to produce change and improve local community and individual family levels of economy.

Poverty and Development

The nature of poverty and why the poor struggle to secure a livelihood has long been debated and while it is well accepted that the provision of schools, health services and other infrastructural facilities are essential, improved resources are not always the solution to the problem of poverty. Mere provision does not ensure access for all. Levels of poverty, income inequalities and asset ownership have a crucial impact on the ability of families and individuals to make use of the services, whether education, health, drinking water, or transport.

The dynamics of a community are often hidden and power structures within it often marginalize the poor and prevent their involvement in development objectives and planning. Development work may, in fact, increase the disparities between the better off and the poorest in communities, particularly where outsiders are not fully conversant with those dynamics. Activities that directly impact the poorest are often contested and the poor need to be empowered to find the means to change the situation. Village leaders are normally the ones who will or will not allow development to occur and the needs of the most vulnerable are often neglected. Social relations dictate entitlements to resources, particularly during difficult times (e.g. access to the water, to food and areas of the forest). Poorer people in communities need substantial support to withstand the pressure of the landed poor, the moneylenders and the community leaders, all of whom have an interest in keeping the poor reliant on them. *"Empowering the poor to enable them to participate in the institutional processes"* is as essential as providing means of security (Turton 2000). A change in attitude is essential if the poorest are not to be denied access to amenities.

The following are some of the factors which need to be taken into consideration when dealing with development in poverty situations:
- High rates of interest, chronic indebtedness, bonding of both land and labour by moneylenders. Control of the informal credit, transport, and contracts, all of which tend to be exploitative.
- Control by the powerful over seasonal migration; for example, little money is left from payments for work after deductions for transport, food and accommodation.
- What happens in disputes? What are the penalties?
- What percentage of people own what percentage of the land; how much land is mortgaged because the owners cannot afford to plant it? What are the rental and sharecropping arrangements, which reduce the incentive for many small and marginal farmers to raise productivity?
- When the rains fail, there are no resources to fall back on. *"Distress sales of land, livestock and other assets are gradually reducing people's capacity to respond to variations in rainfall."* (Turton ibid) When natural calamity strikes, government assistance is usually available but even here

exploitation occurs.
- In the more remote areas government staffing levels are insufficient to monitor and support development.

Thus the idea that projects and interventions will eradicate poverty through community development has been criticised. The benefits of development projects usually go to the better off landowning farmers because most development is land based. A study by the Overseas Development Institute (ODI), London, suggests that *"most schemes have had more impact on their relatively rich clients than on the poorer ones"* (Marr 1999). As well, projects and schemes generally have less impact in remote rural areas, which tend to be the poorer areas and this seems to be true of the tribal regions of AP. Some in these communities may benefit, but the poorest are usually those who continue to be neglected. Unless non-land based development activities are implemented, landless labourers will be largely untouched by development programmes. The poor need to be involved in any project from the start, identifying needs and preparing the design, as well as actively participant in its implementation, using the many strategies they have developed themselves for overcoming poverty.

Projects targeted directly at the poor may have the greatest impact, but benefit a limited number of people, whereas those that target communities affect more people, but often with the side-effect of marginalising the poorest (Cox and Healey 1998). That historical, political and social relations contribute to the complexity of the nature of poverty enabling *"a small, powerful minority to deprive the disempowered majority of their entitlements"* (ibid) is now a well established nostrum in the field of international development. However, although there may be some understanding of the poverty situations in most countries with which donor agencies partner, not all acknowledge this or attempt to change the status quo. Few governments in developing countries have pro-poor strategies in place. India, in fact, does and the Government of Andhra Pradesh (GoAP) has *"already recognised that an approach based solely on natural resource or agriculture is not sufficient for broad-based rural development and in particular for meeting the needs of the poor"* (Turton 2000:18). Current policy is to decentralise development activities with greater involvement of local NGOs and community organisations. Even so, as Turton suggests, *"there is little evidence that development agencies and donors can influence those underlying causes of poverty rooted in the power structures."*

Thus, as for the tribal communities of India, economic growth in a community does not necessarily mean poverty reduction for all. Meeting the basic needs of the poor and improving their income is not sufficient; the poor need to be empowered and a pro-poor strategy, fully supported by the government, is required. Poverty-reducing interventions take time and require flexible solutions. Every situation is different and change will not happen quickly; several decades will pass before the required changes become of the accepted social and political structure. It is here, however, that an organisation such as AASSAV, a local tribal society, will better understand the local dynamics and more successfully implement change than any outsider.

Local economy

Many changes have occurred for the tribal people in the Paderu agency area and for some, conditions are improving. At the start of the Adivasi Oriya language project in the early 1970s the people of the region had very little actual cash. Little by little, more money has been coming in, some as a direct result of the project and some as an indirect result as educated and trained individuals have been able to get jobs with the government as teachers, or with the police, or in Visakhapatnam (the nearest city), and are sending money home to their families. The people of Hattaguda and other local villages state that they are now better off.

In the past people had only one or two changes of clothes, but now many have much more. Cinema, television and newspapers are available. Cooking used to be done with earthenware vessels. The few families who cooked with aluminium or brass pots were considered wealthy. Now earthenware is hardly used, except in the interior villages.

Primary education has always been free, but more children are now attending secondary schools as parents are able and willing to pay for them to do so. They have begun to see that education is one of the most important factors in economic improvement.

For those who have land, a cash crop will bring in money, but for those who do not there is little chance of employment. People of the interior villages, particularly, have much less opportunity to work for money. They would, and still do, sell firewood, vegetables they have grown, or hire themselves out as labourers. Many do not have enough food for the whole year and malnourishment is widespread.

Education

Telugu medium schools have been in the tribal region since 1949. A number of people close to the townships attended these schools to grade five. A small percentage of those graduated from 10th grade. Later, the boys of a few of the more wealthy families attended English Medium convent schools. More recently the Integrated Tribal Development Agency (ITDA), the local government agency for tribal welfare, established multigrade, single-classroom schools in villages. Tribal tenth grade graduates have been given training with a newly developed curriculum more relevant to rural and tribal life. The curriculum is still in Telugu, but the teacher is able to translate into the local language if the children have problems understanding. These schools are often more successful at keeping their students and their teachers than the Telugu medium state schools. In 2004, a curriculum using Adivasi Oriya, the mother tongue or link language of these communities, was developed with a transition to second language (Telugu). This is proving to be a more positive educational experience for tribal children in the primary grades as it builds on the knowledge they bring to school of their language, culture and environment.

Those who have studied at an English Medium school often receive greater respect in the community. The vice president of AASSAV, who attended a convent school, describes how he is made to sit on a good chair when visiting, how his advice is sought and how he is requested to mediate between villagers and doctors, even at two or three o'clock in the morning, if there is a serious medical problem. But this can be a double-edged asset. This same vice president is aware that his education and status create a social distancing and he feels that he cannot get as close to people in the villages as he would like. His own son, who also attends the convent school, has gained in confidence and because of his education his peers also give him more respect.

There are often no jobs for these educated young people. Having no job and not being prepared for local labour, boredom and material need become endemic. Gangs of tribal youths raid property, stealing vegetables and other crops. Although they come mainly from Orissa, similar problems have been reported in the AP agency area.

Transport and Communication

Hattaguda itself was built as a model village and given new houses, a bore well, road and other facilities by the government in 1960. The location of a village, infrastructural facilities, such as transport and electricity, accessibility of the village, and extent of mobility among villagers to and from the village, all have a bearing on the nature and extent of development in the area.   Roads, homes, education, electrification, irrigation and so on, are basic to the economic development of the tribal Agency area and the Government recognises this in its attempts to make adequate provision.

There are three major tarred roads that lead into the Paderu Agency from the coastal plains.   All of these converge at the district headquarters of Visakhapatnam.   There are several tarred roads within the Agency connecting the towns of Chintapalli, Paderu, Munchingput and Araku. Besides these there are numerous gravel and dirt roads.

A government bus service runs between the Agency townships and some villages, and to the coastal cities. Jeeps operating as taxis ply these roads venturing further into the interior on unmade up roads. Goods and services can be transported in and out of the Agency throughout the year, at a price.   A passenger train provides a daily service from Visakhapatnam to the Agency at Araku and beyond.

Electricity has been made available to all of the administrative townships in the Agency and to many villages.   There are still breakdowns, but the supply is improving.   Postal and telephone services are available from all administrative centres within the Agency, with the postal service reaching every village and hamlet.

Tourism

Tourism has resulted in more interest in tribal culture and society and the people themselves are beginning to see their own ways as valuable, and worth preserving. A museum of tribal culture has been established in Araku Valley and dancers and musicians perform for tourists, usually on a Sunday when tourists come up for a day. There is even some overnight tourism now, since the facilities, particularly developed by AP Tourism, are improving in the area. How much this impacts the tribal community in terms of improved living conditions is debatable: although young tribals are being trained and employed in the new facilities, very few, if any, are in management positions.

Conclusion

The people of this region live in remote and difficult circumstances, often with no electricity or running water, walking some distance to find sources of water from a spring or well and, as the forest retreats, having to search further afield for firewood. Access to services such as health and education is limited and even where they are available, quality is inadequate and the people are hampered by poverty from using them. However, there are signs of positive improvement in their life circumstances as indicated in the following chapters.

TOPICS FOR DISCUSSION

1. 'The impact of national and global economic and social change on the rural tribal communities of India (such as these of the Paderu Agency in AP) has so far been predominantly negative.' Do you agree or disagree?

2. Should tourism be encouraged in tribal areas?

3. In what ways can tribal people be proactive in the preservation of their traditional values?

4. In the radical changes beginning to disrupt traditional life-styles, how may tribal people ensure that their knowledge of the forest is not lost but rather put to good use more widely? How might it be possible to safeguard their 'rights' to remuneration for such potentially valuable 'intellectual property'?

5. How might the perpetuation of tribal identity be ensured?

6. What aspects of traditional tribal values ought to be challenged?

CHAPTER 2

Building a local organisation

In 1965 the state government established the Integrated Tribal Development Agency (ITDA) specifically for tribal development. Up until that time there had been little development activity in the Araku Valley and no NGO had worked in the area.

Language and literacy development

In 1970 with the arrival of Uwe and Elke Gustafsson working with SIL International, the foundations of a literacy programme were laid. One of the first objectives was to develop a viable writing system for the language and, drawing on data from contacts in the villages of the area, the Gustafssons began work. At first everything was written in phonetic script, but after developing an orthography at training workshops in Visakhaptanam and Nepal using the Telugu script, a writing system was validated by Andhra University. The Telugu script was chosen as it is the script of the state language of the region and in order to function in the wider society, Telugu is essential: most education and development opportunities require Telugu.

Two local mother tongue speakers, Kilo Pratap, son of the Panchayat President, and Golori Ram were invited as language assistants to linguistic workshops at Andhra University in Visakhapatnam and at Tribhuvan University in Kathmandu. Pratap was illiterate, but he was socially superior to Ram and understood much about the culture. He took this position very seriously, but the real writer and language assistant was Ram. Hundreds of stories were collected and anthropological notes made about dancing, festivals, and customs. Before these language development efforts started, the tribal people had taken little interest in their own language and culture, but now their perceptions changed and they became strongly motivated to write all their early experiences so that their existence and customs did not get lost to memory. Pratap continues even now in his old age to dictate to a writer all he knows about the culture: the customs, the forest trees, fruits and medicines, tribal experiences and so on.

The enthusiasm and commitment of the group of language assistants,

which eventually numbered seven, is evidenced by the fact that they
would often work together until 9pm at night. Raghunadh, one of the
original team and later president of AASSAV said:

> *We worked on literacy until 9pm, and after that we would sit*
> *around the fire in someone's home and have discussions. We*
> *were wondering why only a few people were being reached. We*
> *wanted to reach more...* (Interview, 2002)

In 1974, after four years of intensive linguistic research (Gustafsson
1991:27), a 120-page text concordance, a phonological study, a
grammar and a 4000-word vocabulary were produced. By 1979
primers, graded readers and post-primer materials in Adivasi Oriya,
with Telugu translations, bridging materials for teaching Telugu, had
been completed and test classes conducted. After ten years an
Adivasi-Oriya – Telugu – English dictionary was compiled and
published by the Central Institute of Indian Languages, Mysore.

In 1979 the District Collector provided twelve literacy centres where
the team ran the bi-lingual programme. These were working well, but
during the following year, the National Adult Education Programme
(NAEP) began literacy work in Telugu medium and the centres were
taken over by them. The Project had no choice but to terminate the
Adivasi Oriya - Telugu literacy programme. After many apparently
fruitless visits to district and state government offices to secure
permission to continue, there was a turnaround when the NAEP
suddenly requested the Project to restart the bilingual programme in 30
centres. And so in 1983 the government of Andhra Pradesh gave
permission for the *Adivasi Oriya – Telugu* literacy books to be used by
the project in teaching literacy classes. To gain government approval
learning Telugu was essential. The literacy programme, including all
the material productions, was funded by CIDA (Canadian International
Development Agency), together with the provincial governments of
Alberta, Saskatchewan and Manitoba, as well as LEAD, (Literacy,
Education and Development), AASSAV's partner NGO based in
Calgary, Canada.

The work carried on in this manner for three years. Village leaders
would encourage attendance at classes in their own way:

> *"When we came at night, supervising the programmes, the*
> *village elders would shout and tell the children and young adults*
> *to get to school and drum up all the younger children. They*
> *would all stand around, "Now read this, how can you not study?*
> *You come more regularly."* (Interview Gustafsson 2002)

The younger generation attended school at times so knew how to read and write a little in Telugu already, but for adults the consequences of becoming literate were very significant. Non literate adults were looked down upon. Older people said how embarrassing it was for them at the government offices:

> *"We have to give our thumb print and we don't know what for, and they tell us something we have to do it. Now, no more, and we can even read."*

One man who was a bondservant, learned literacy and because of his abilities got a job at AASSAV, something which could never have happened before.

Kilo Pratap, one of the original team members, recalls the early days:

> *[The programme] went out into other villages ... The people learned to read and write and got jobs and it is all due to this literacy. The language written was so beneficial. It was good that people could learn in their mother tongue... it was very good and to learn Telugu from this. Many people went on to school or to study privately to prepare for exams and so many have passed 10th grade. They were young adults, but the chance for school had finished, and in many cases there was no school. So that helped them very much.* (Interview 2002)

Over 11,000 Adivasi adults from more than 600 villages became fully literate in Adivasi Oriya using this programme. Many of these also became literate in Telugu.

At the same time, the District Collector (DC) asked for the Adivasi Oriya – Telugu literacy books to be introduced to primary schools as a pilot project. The Gustafssons and their Adivasi co-workers were given several schools in which to test the programme. It worked well in only one school where the teacher was cooperative. A survey showed that the children who had learned through the mother tongue were far ahead of those who had begun to learn in Telugu only. But the teachers' union was very annoyed about its introduction. They said it would create too much work and teachers were not able to cope with it. They complained to the DC and since the Teachers' Union is very strong in India, there was nothing more he could do to implement a bilingual programme in the schools. One of the main problems at that time was that most teachers were Telugu speakers and did not speak or understand the tribal language and culture. Since 2000 however more tribal teachers, most of whom are 10th grade graduates, have been trained as teachers and in 2004 a new mother tongue programme with bridging to Telugu, based in tribal language and culture was introduced and accepted with enthusiasm.

The Literacy Programme

From the beginning of the literacy programme, the use of the mother tongue had always been regarded as the most effective way to become literate. Even literacy in the dominant language was best achieved through initial literacy in the mother tongue.

This is the view that has been gaining ground elsewhere amongst literacy experts. As far back as 1951 a group of specialists at UNESCO had strongly recommended the *"use of the vernacular language for Fundamental Education as being the only effective and correct pedagogical vehicle of teaching."* This was reinforced in 2002 when UNESCO proclaimed the principle that *"mother tongue instruction is essential for initial education and literacy..."* (UNESCO 2002:31).

> *Learning to talk in your mother tongue is an arduous task. Learning to read and write in that language is even more difficult. But learning to read and write in a language other than your own is an experience that requires an enormous capacity for endurance"* (Metshazi 1987:52).

A person only has to learn to read once; the skills can be transferred to the second language.

In multilingual situations, particularly those in minority language contexts, such as this is, there is now broad agreement that mother tongue acquisition is the basis for competence in second and third languages.

> *Students who have learned to read in their mother tongue learn to read in a second language more quickly than do those who are first taught to read in the second language. ... In terms of academic learning skills ... students taught to read in their mother tongue acquire such skills more quickly'* (Mehrotra, S. 1998: Quoted in UNESCO 2002).

> *... The first language is essential for the initial teaching of reading and for comprehension of subject matter. It is the necessary foundation for the cognitive development upon which acquisition of the second language is based'* (Dutcher, N. and Tucker, G.R. 1996)

> *A strong foundation in mother tongue and a good bridge into the second language is required for successful literacy and education*

programmes (Malone, S. Training course in Hyderabad 2005).

Some have argued that the importance of the first language goes far beyond skills and cultural knowledge and beyond cognitive and affective benefits. The first language is the *"very life blood of human self-awareness"* (Metshazi 1987). It is the carrier of a person's identity, deeply intertwined with personality.

The general conclusions of research and experience are that an education which utilizes local languages and cultures is beneficial both to the individual and to the communities.

- Learning to read in a language which is familiar is more effective and easier than learning to read in an unfamiliar language.

- This sets up a 'virtuous cycle' in which motivation is better sustained and students are less likely to lose heart and drop out.

- Second language learning is more successful if founded on solid first language foundation.

- Reading and writing skills as well as new concepts can be transferred from one language to another.

Besides providing a more effective education and a smoother transition to state and national languages, a literacy programme which values local languages and gives respect to local cultures develops self-esteem and cultural identity among the people, helping thus to maintain local languages and cultures. The literacy programme instigated by the Gustafssons in partnership with committed local people has notably exemplified these values and goals.

By contrast, most reports on literacy achievement today, whether in minority or majority language situations, state that adult literacy programmes fail. Usually these failed programmes have been developed and introduced by outsiders – governments and NGOs. They have failed because there is no real knowledge of the community, the content having been developed and written with no local involvement. It cannot therefore reflect in a deep and vibrant way the thought forms, life patterns and historical memories of the tribal group. Furthermore, without strong partnership with the local community there tends to be no continuity and no real literacy backup without which gains in literacy may be largely lost again.

It is now generally recognised that literacy programmes should be tailored to meet the needs of target groups and be introduced at a time when they perceive the need for themselves (Rogers 2000). To develop specific programmes that meet the needs of a particular group, however, requires a high level of teaching skill and experience and it cannot be expected that the teachers in the villages, who are just a few grades up from the learners, will be competent to do this. Thus a structured programme has to be provided.

The programme developed in the Adivasi Oriya community was completely culturally based, and produced together with local community members. The assistants were from village schools, which meant that they could only just read and write. But when they looked at the result of their efforts, they knew their people could easily become literate with such materials: it was comprehensible and accessible. And they were right - in practice the new literacy students were eager to learn and to continue learning.

The literacy programme placed emphasis on the participation and support of the village elders and of the Adivasi community as a whole. The major object was to enable adults (usually aged between 15-35, although younger people often joined the classes) to achieve literacy in Telugu, using mother tongue initially and bridging to Telugu. The programme contained 71 lessons in Primers I and II based on the Adivasi Oriya language and its associated Readers I and II, and then Primer III (bridging to Telugu) with its associated Reader III. There were also several post-primer readers and other books (which had been published). All lessons and post-primer readers had been translated into Telugu in a diglot version. To support and encourage the newly literate to put their new skills into immediate use, government brochures and pamphlets and development information were translated and published and a monthly newsletter was issued.

The lessons took place in the evenings for 2 hours, 6 days a week for 10 months of the year. At the end of the course an examination in Telugu could be taken. Successful candidates were awarded a certificate that was recognised by the Government and highly prized. An extra page which tested knowledge of the Telugu language in more depth was added at one point, but few had any great knowledge of the Telugu language, fewer still amongst those who lived in the interior villages. Most men can handle Telugu in spoken form for the purposes they need, such as the market, but as Cummins (1979) points out, the distinction between conversational fluency or "basic interpersonal communicative skills" (BICS) and the academic ability in second language, "cognitive academic language proficiency" (CALPS) are very different. Approximately two years of exposure to the second language is required to attain a functional level (BICS) whereas at least five years is required to attain an ability equivalent to native speakers in academic aspects of the second language (Collier 1987:617; Cummins 1981:132). Since the adult tribal learners need encouragement above all and the extra paper was feeding a sense of failure, this second test was withdrawn. *"Adult learners once discouraged, for whatever reason, are not likely to try again."* (Final Report 2000:27).

Organisers (or teachers) were responsible for the village Literacy Centres. They were approved and monitored by the village elders. Trained supervisors visited the centres each month. The team were out 3-4 nights a week making the rounds of the centres. They graded each learner, met with the organisers and monitored progress. They wanted to learn what problems there were with the programme. Gustafsson commented that

> *"it was so wonderful to see how the people got on. There was not a word in the primer that they stumbled over. They knew the meaning. They only had to put the syllables together and they had it."* (Interview 2002)

This was because they were learning in a language they understood and with content they were interested in. They were not attempting to learn two things at once; literacy and a second language.

Organisers and supervisors had a monthly meeting at Hattaguda when administrative and professional matters were dealt with. Record keeping was an important feature and all data was kept on Progress Report Forms. There was a strong focus on punctuality and standards. Achievements of both supervisors and learners were also recognised and rewarded at special functions.

In his 1987 report Professor J Cairns, then of Guelph University in Canada, stated:

> *"This is a model of what a literacy project should be. It exhibits a high level of professionalism in almost every aspect, and is well worthy of study, emulation and further support."*

This was high praise indeed as the conditions under which they had to operate were not easy. The tribal people themselves were conducting the programme and although they used local organisational patterns as far as possible to support and encourage learners, many new skills among the supervisors and organisers needed to be developed. Besides this, tribal people, marginalized from mainstream Indian society, live in isolated villages often not accessible by road. Communication and

travel were both difficult. Electricity was often not available and
where it was, there were frequent cuts. To operate a programme
successfully in such conditions required resilience and patience as well
as careful planning, management and supervision.

Adult Education and Development Centres

As a deliberate follow-up to the literacy programme, centres were set
up to encourage the utilization and support the retention of literacy.
These were intended to be a continuation of the literacy programme,
moving on to adult education and development without which it was
likely that new literates would lose their new abilities.

It was intended that the leaders of these centres would take on a wider
role than that of an organiser of literacy classes. Their diverse
responsibilities read more like that of a development worker:
- extension worker for AASSAV
- adult literacy supervisor
- community school programme supervisor
- adult literacy surveyor
- newsletter distributor
- collection of written stories/articles from new literates
- organising meetings with government officers
- supervising the tailoring work of the ITDA/AASSAV trained
  tribal women
- supervising the Family Rabbit Farms
- community health promoter
- village librarian
- social forestry promoter

In practice these centres operated as a base from which the leader
connected with about 20 surrounding villages, reaching 500-600
villages in total. The centres were used from the start for activities
such as radio listening, where, on their own initiative, people met to
discuss issues they had heard about. But they did not operate fully as
intended until the time when AASSAV's relationship with Naandi and
CARE developed and income-generating activities created a need for
them.

Guru groups

Guru groups were run by successful new literates and were set up to
provide a second opportunity for those who did not achieve full
literacy in the regular programme. Some also attended to improve
further their skills either in Adivasi Oriya or in Telugu. The guru
groups provided an informal and supportive environment for the
learners and ensured that a greater number of learners actually became

literate.

The Newsletter

Beginning in 1984, a bilingual Educational Newsletter was produced and printed monthly by AASSAV. Adivasi Oriya was printed in one column with Telugu in the other. The translation was done at the headquarters, and was then sent to a professor at Nagarjuna University, Guntur to check. Copies were sent to all government departments, the District Collector, the Superintendent of Police and the Project Officer at ITDA. The purpose of the newsletter was to disseminate post-literacy materials for new literates and to serve as an educational tool in providing articles and stories on relevant development issues. Stories and articles written by Adivasis themselves were published as were articles by government departments and educational institutions, focusing on issues relating to health and nutrition, on women in development and on the environment. Some of the subjects covered included agriculture, horticulture, animal husbandry, coffee cultivation, sericulture, education, health, general development, biographies of local lives, bee keeping, and mushroom cultivation. The newsletter was a vital tool, serving the dual purpose of encouraging reading (and even writing) and spreading useful information relating to development. Publishing ceased in 1999 when funding dried up.

Women and literacy

Within the tribal areas of Andhra Pradesh, female literacy levels are below 10% and female school dropouts amounted to 70%. The difference in achievement between male and female participants in the programme was likewise striking and reflected the background trend. Table 2.1 shows the results over three years.

In all cases the percentage of men attending was much higher than women. In each year the literacy achievement rate for males was near or above 90%; the equivalent rate for women was 10% or below. The reasons given for this unequal state of affairs include the following:

- Women face being ridiculed by men. Husbands do not value literacy for their wives and society says that women do not have brains capable of learning. Younger married women often live with mothers-in-law who are non-literate and may resent their daughters-in-law becoming literate.

Keeping it local: change and devleopment in an
Indian tribal community

Table 2.1

Male-Female Literacy Percentages from 1991 to 1993					
	1991		1992		1993	
	Male	Female	Male	Female	Male	Female
Attendance	68.0	32.0	82.0	18.0	71.8	28.2
Literacy*	95.4	4.6	92.7	7.3	89.6	10.4

*This figure represents the % of those who attended who gained literacy

- There are no separate classes for women and there are few women teachers or supervisors. Although separate classes were tried, they were not successful. Men did not like the idea that women learned alone and wanted to attend the same classes.
- Women have very little time to do all their household duties and outside work. In May and June women do much of the planting; from July to September they do the weeding and after that they are involved more than men in harvesting. Many of those who enrol have young children and babies to look after.
- The classes are held at inappropriate times for women. Early evening when the classes are held is the time when women are normally busy cooking and working in their homes.
- It was also suggested that women were slower in reaching literacy because they are learning in a male dominated environment. It was felt that the male organisers *"cannot bring themselves to give equal attention to the young female learners"* (Final Report 1990:26).

The table 2.2 reveals the total numbers of male and female literates over all the years of the literacy programme which reveals a very low percentage of women learners: about 7% of the total number of learners. This supports research conducted by Corson in 1993[1] which found that the three groups most marginalised by educational policies and planning are women and girls, the poor and those whose language is not represented in the system. "The injustice is clearly greatest for those who experience all three conditions simultaneously". (UNESCO 2005:2)

In non-literate societies, the battle for competence is often dependent on the individual learner's taking responsibility for her or his own learning which requires a great deal of personal proactivity. Literate societies provide "institutionalised support" (Heath 1984), where various mechanisms for the continuance of literacy have become part of the culture. In newly developing areas a conscious and concerted

---

[1] Quoted in UNESCO 2005

effort needs to put literacy in place as part of the shared cultural resources of the society so that it is not perceived as a marginal phenomenon.

Table 2.2

Year	No of Centres	Literates in Adivasi-Oriya		Literates in Adivasi Oriya and Telugu		Total Literates		Grand Total Literates
		Male	Female	Male	Female	Male	Female	
1983	27	120	4	116	0	236	4	**240**
1984	92	176	14	200	2	376	16	**392**
1985	151	505	12	740	12	1245	24	**1269**
1986	162	308	30	970	14	1278	44	**1322**
1987	None Conducted							
1988	119	200	53	793	48	993	101	**1094**
1989	224	485	32	909	35	1394	67	**1461**
1990	None Conducted							
1991	15	1	1	93	4	94	5	**99**
1992	106	109	22	962	62	1071	84	**1155**
1993	153	317	47	495	47	812	94	**906**
1994	52	205	28	430	21	635	49	**684**
1995	97	295	59	874	103	1169	162	**1331**
1996	96	415	38	677	27	1092	65	**1157**
TOTAL	**1294**	**3136**	**340**	**7259**	**375**	**10395**	**715**	**11110**

While AASSAV itself gives women equal status to men, Adivasi culture does not and there have been very few women members of AASSAV and none at all in the management and executive teams, a fact which is discussed further in chapters 4 and 5. Women need literacy urgently and AASSAV agrees that a special emphasis on eradicating illiteracy among women is necessary. The Evaluation Report 2000 stated that:

> *"Despite the considerable role of women in other project activities, these figures indicate the need for much greater efforts to increase female participation in literacy programming, both in Adivasi-Oriya and Telugu. Since the existing situation is at least partly based on traditional values and perceptions, any significant expansion of women's literacy will require both time and effort."*

UNESCO (2005) also argues for greater emphasis on girls' education, stating that the social and cultural barriers are heavily weighed against females inclusion, but that mother tongue and bilingual education is one of the ways to break down the barriers to participation.

Although the rates have been very low, they are expected to improve, as more emphasis is being placed on literacy for women in micro-enterprise projects, family development projects and self help groups.

The national government has an emphasis on the education of girls, which, it is hoped, will have a long-term impact. AASSAV itself conducted six years of government training for girls from1994 to 2000, which included literacy. 240 girls went through this programme. Although there was no follow-up at the time, these girls were encouraged to join the self-help groups that were being formed in the region. Their training in skills and literacy would be very useful in such groups, particularly in the savings groups at the AASSAV Cooperative Bank[2]. The literate girls would be able to help with the accounting: a capability within the groups to do this for themselves is vital to avoid getting cheated.

During 2003, which saw the beginning of the Naandi Coffee Project and the CARE STEP (Sustainable Tribal Empowerment Programme), many more women and girls began to attend the literacy classes, but these were often the children of the families, not the wives. So, while the goal of literacy for all age groups is commendable, it is the rising generation who have the greater interest and the current generation of non-literate women is unlikely to be significantly touched.

The impact of literacy

It is said that a non-literate person often views the outside world with suspicion. The difficulties (poverty, social exclusion, limited knowledge of life beyond the tribe and so on) experienced by tribal people are further compounded by their inability to read or write the official language. They are shy, rarely approaching government officials, because they cannot read handouts or sign their names. Self-evidently this deters them from taking advantage of development programmes. Non-literate people are very reluctant to leave their cultural or language area unless they are in the company of a literate person. Even travelling by bus within their own language area is a strain for non-literate persons. They are familiar with stories of tribal people who have gone to a city or travelled between townships who have been misguided or overcharged. They also hear stories of non-literate people buying things that are not what they seemed to be. Once literacy has been achieved the learner is no longer embarrassed, but acquires confidence, has less fear of the unknown and will venture out, more able now to defend himself against exploitation.

It was not easy, however, to establish literacy classes at first as most tribals did not see the benefits and did not want to learn. It was only

---

[2] See Chapter 4:61 MACS Bank

after the success of some centres that more local people became interested and motivation increased. One of the major motivating factors for learning was that the object was competence in reading and writing Telugu. It is through Telugu that individuals, families and communities are able to take advantage of the development projects that are being offered. It is through Telugu that the tribal people are able to access the benefits of mainstream Indian society and contribute to the nation as a whole. Illiteracy is, therefore, often a barrier to an individual's development. Training programmes in agriculture, horticulture and soil conservation are open to the non-literate but others are not. The AASSAV certificate of Adivasi Oriya and Telugu Literacy has been accepted for training programmes such as carpentry, masonry and tailoring.

Some who completed the literacy programme went on with their schooling afterwards since the government accepted the certificate as a valid qualification to continue. Younger graduates of the literacy programme were accepted into Grade 6 at government boarding schools. Many of these were then were able to get government and other jobs. They in their turn sent their children to school, built block instead of mud houses, bought equipment to improve their agricultural productivity and thus material possessions were gradually built up. In this way the literacy programme has brought incremental economic development to the community.

By 2000, 11,110 tribal people had graduated from the literacy programme. Of these 10,395 were men, 715 were women. 3136 men and 340 women achieved literacy in Adivasi Oriya only. 7259 men and 375 women also achieved literacy in Telugu. The imbalance between men and women is marked. Even though the positive impact of literacy for women on a whole family is significant, affecting family health, nutrition, sanitation, children's welfare in general and their achievement in school, local attitudes towards women have been slow to change.

In 2003, however, many of the younger generation attend literacy classes; often they are under 20 and some are as young as twelve. More girls have also been attending with female learners almost one third of the total number of learners (see Table 2.3).

Table 2.3

Adivasi Oriya-Telugu Adult Education Programme   **Monthly Evaluation: August 2003**

Lesson	1-10		11-20		21-30		31-40		41-50		51-60		61-70		71-80		81-94		Total No of Participants		Grand total M F
	M	F	M	F	M	F	M	F	M	F	M	F	M	F	M	F	M	F	M	F	
	80	119	62	54	41	24	81	39	114	23	64	13	63	19	183	48	65	4	753	343	1096

During the last few years, increasing activity in the villages with women's cooperative groups resulted in women now perceiving their own need for literacy skills. With the emphasis on girls' education and training by the government the attitudes of men have begun to change families are less likely to say that girls do not need education. Women and girls are therefore gaining in self-confidence and ridicule is no longer a factor. There has only ever been one woman organiser, but there is a good chance that may also change in years to come as more educated women become available locally.

Adivasis Oriya is the lingua franca of the region, but for some it is not their mother tongue. Where learners attending a literacy programme who are mother tongue speakers of one of the other local tribal languages, such as the Konda, it often takes two years rather than one to become literate.

Literacy and Development

This programme continued for three years, with funding from CIDA, LEAD, three Canadian provincial governments (Alberta, Manitoba and Saskatchewan) and some private donors. Then in 1987, Professor John C Cairns visited the project to write an evaluation report for the Canadian funders which was to change the direction of the work. He suggested that literacy should be integrated with community development projects in order to establish the economic self-sufficiency of the entire project in the future. Cairns argued that

> "*in too many literacy projects the achievement of literacy is seen as an end in itself, rather than a means to further development and improvement of living conditions. In such cases long term sustainability and impact are marginal.*" (Evaluation Report 1997:2)

Gustafsson, in the early days of the literacy work, had always regarded literacy as a tool to overcoming barriers to development and it has always been one of AASSAV's central aims, but as Cairns also noted

> "*literacy is an essential, but insufficient component for development (nevertheless) if we ignore it, we have great difficulty solving other development issues*" (Evaluation Report 1985).

Rogers (2001) also argues that the relationship between literacy and development may not be causal at all, but rather some kind of associative relationship. Wagner (1993) suggests that it is not a simple relationship, but that literacy, culture and development are interconnected in complex ways. Literacy as a factor in economic, social (individual or community) and cultural change is dependent on a number of other interrelated factors.

After some discussion with local leaders and government officials, a tribal society was formed and registered, providing a legal association that could work officially on development projects with government, NGOs and INGOs. The progress of the newly formed society and the relationship between development and literacy is described in the subsequent chapters of this book; however, the new organisation had drastic effects on literacy.

One major difficulty after beginning income-generating projects is revealed by quote from the Final Report (2000:28):

> *"We had a very good team of supervisors until we began with the income-generating projects. We just had to re-assign some of the better educated men to be trained for other skills, giving them the opportunity of permanent employment. Several other supervisors left our project for better paid government jobs. The supervision techniques and monitoring/internal evaluation remained, but the staff to use these were drastically reduced and also less qualified.*

The inclusion of a literacy component as part of the new Family Coffee Development Project was debated long and hard before Naandi, the new partner and funding organisation, agreed. AASSAV argued that to become fully self-reliant, one needs literacy; the Naandi Foundation, however, stressed the importance of economic stability as a basis for self-reliance. They wanted to remove the literacy component from the proposal, but eventually reluctantly consented and in 2003, 68 new literacy centres were opened. These ran for one year.

The CARE programme, STEP, is operating in a different way and the implementation of projects depends on the aspirations of the community. The range of development programmes that can be offered includes literacy and education, but the demand for such classes has to come from the community. AASSAV will only run these classes as mother tongue with transition to Telugu.

Conclusions

CIDA funded the literacy programmes from their inception until 1989 when the Society was formed. Following this CIDA continued to provide funding for both literacy and development programmes, but the focus was now on becoming a self-financing and self-managing organisation, and in practice, in the confusion that followed funding gaps, the literacy work ceased to be a central activity. The change in focus to development led to two results for AASSAV. On the one hand, there was an increased need for literacy, while on the other hand the ability to maintain programmes was reduced owing to the redirection of personnel, finances and time away from literacy activities. AASSAV's capacity to deliver literacy was reduced by the seemingly more important and pressing occupations of income generation.

What then is, or should be, the relationship between educational aspects (adult literacy, functional education projects), development work (clean water, health) and income generation? A holistic community development surely should include them all, developing human potential, a better environment and economic opportunity. Literacy, education, economic development, health, and environment - all are important in improving the standard of living of the individual, the family and of the community. The remainder of this book looks at the ways in which the tribal organisation grew - the struggles, the successes and failures; and the place of literacy in the process.

TOPICS FOR DISCUSSION

1. Do you agree that a person's first language is the *'very life blood of human self-awareness'*?

2. Comment on the process adopted here of developing a written language in Adivasi Oriya and its subsequent use in literacy classes. Is it a good model?

3. What impact does the acquisition of literacy have a) on an individual b) on a community?

4. How can the newly literate who are also living in isolated communities maintain their skill and how can they be supported in this?

5. What hindrances stand in the way of tribal women becoming literate and how might these be overcome?

6. *'Literacy is an essential but insufficient component for development (nevertheless) if we ignore it, we have great difficulty solving other development issues.'* Suggest ways in which successful development depends on literacy, and ways in which literacy might promote development.

CHAPTER 3

What Kind of Development?

"Development is ... a complex and slow-moving process involving people on the one hand and the factors of production and organisation on the other. It is obviously not a simple matter of an investment project here and a training programme there.... Perhaps the whole concept of development programmes is wrong. Perhaps development workers need to settle down to working patiently over time, directly with people, facilitating and supporting initiatives arising from the ambitions and priorities of individuals, groups and the community at large. Perhaps then we would begin to see the emergence of sustainable development processes powered by people themselves."

Chambers 1983:39

A Change in Focus

In 1987, following Cairns' report and a change in policy, CIDA insisted that a move into income generating work was essential if the funds were to continue. CIDA used two main arguments to support their decision: firstly, linking literacy to development would increase the benefit to the tribal people in their efforts towards becoming self-reliant and secondly, income-generating projects should fund the literacy project so that this work would become self-financing. The Final Report (1990) stated:

> *All businesses established will be for profit which will then be used for the support of the adult literacy and education work among the tribal people."* (9)

The group of co-workers who had helped with the study and analysis of the language and who had written and implemented the literacy programme had formed a committee which managed the literacy programme. This committee met to discuss the ultimatum and the link between literacy and development. A monthly newsletter had been published in which articles from the Telugu Agriculture Magazine had been translated, but a survey showed that although some people had implemented some of the suggestions given, the effect was not great. They began to understand that in circumstances of poverty, marginalisation and oppression, literacy alone would rarely lead to development; something more would have to be done. The poor and marginalized needed practical support as they made attempts to access the development processes available through government and other agencies. The committee however did not want to concentrate only on development projects as this would leave their primary objective unfulfilled. They believed that it was necessary to continue with literacy, adult education and discussion groups. For example, while the people needed to be encouraged to grow things that were nutritious they also needed to be encouraged not to sell it all. They obtained good money for crops such as lentils and peas, and so would retain little for themselves. Families were eating only small amounts of nutritious food and were suffering the consequences in terms of poor health. Knowledge in the areas of health and nutrition would be taught through the adult education groups.

In the end the literacy team felt that if they wanted to continue to help their people, they would have to comply with CIDA's demands and become a development *and* literacy organisation. Managing the literacy programme had equipped the team with the confidence and experience needed to facilitate this expansion.

The emergence of AASSAV

The literacy management committee approached the Project Officer (PO) of the Integrated Tribal Development Agency (ITDA) to discuss the idea with him. The PO is the head of ITDA, responsible for all government development activities within the Tribal Agency area. The offices were in Paderu, Visakapatnam District, 50 kilometres away from Hattaguda. The literacy work had taken place in the development area under the PO's control, the committee always informing the PO of developments and wherever possible had worked with the government's programmes. They wished to continue this positive relationship, so early in 1988 the leaders of the *Adivasi Oriya – Telugu Literacy Programme* spent an evening with the PO in his home. He was very positive about the new suggestion and recommended that they immediately form and register a society. This would allow the government to work directly with the Society in development projects. One employee from the ITDA office was deputed to them and with the full agreement of the Adivasi leaders a Society was formed.

The seven people on the Language and Literacy Management

Committee went to Visakapatnam to register the society. Obtaining the various permissions necessary to establish the organisation was a long and arduous process. No-one understood at the time just how much work they had committed themselves to (Gustafsson 1991).

Registration took place on 17 April 1988 when the Society was named Adivasi Samaskruthika Sangam, Araku Valley (*The Tribal Cultural Society of Araku Valley*). On 13 March 1992 the Society was re-registered and the name was changed to Adivasi Abhivruddi Samskruthika Sangam, Araku Valley, AASSAV (*The Tribal Development and Cultural Society Araku Valley*) as this title was more appropriate to it purpose, goals and activities.

Structure, purpose and goals of AASSAV

Thus AASSAV was established as a Society, under Indian government regulations, to work for the general development and literacy of the Adivasi people in the Paderu Agency of Visakhapatnan District. The Paderu Agency covers eleven mandals, in six of which Adivasi Oriya is spoken as the mother tongue: Anantagiri, Araku Valley, Dumbriguda, Ukumpetta, Peddabaylu and Munchingput.

It was founded as a secular, charitable and voluntary organisation to serve the educational, economic, health, environmental, cultural and social development particularly of the Adivasi-Oriya language group. The management committee of the Society consisted only of tribal people. Gustafsson's role[1] became one of coordinator, advisor and resource person.

The Society was set up not as an isolated organisation but as part of the whole development process for the Adivasis, which the Government of India and the Government of Andhra Pradesh had initiated, and which happened mainly through the Office of the PO of the ITDA, Paderu. ITDA offered a variety of development programmes including health, education, particularly primary schools and girls' education, agricultural support and a food for work scheme. AASSAV, being a tribal organisation, with knowledge of the region, and understanding the language and culture, could offer support to the government in implementing many of these programmes.

AASSAV's goal was to help the tribal people re-establish themselves and improve their economic situation and life chances following the partial destruction of their traditional way of life - their dependency

---

[1] See Chapter 4: 85 The Role of an Expatriate

on the forest. The aim was the comprehensive development of the person, family and community; literacy, functional education and community development were goals equal with economic development. Individual and community autonomy, or self-reliance, was to be achieved through both literacy and community development, with the assistance of government agencies, NGOs and INGOs as well as the families and communities who were partners of the development process.

AASSAV was established as an indigenous organisation so that the Adivasis themselves could be full participants in the development process. It was intended that they should be partners, beneficiaries and owners of the development process and its results. In addition AASSAV provided employment to Adivasi men and women in its literacy, development and income generating projects as well as in its administration. The Memorandum of Association provides that only those registered as tribals can be members. The Final Report (1990) stated

> *"The businesses themselves will employ only tribal men and women and thus give opportunity for an income, and guarantee a better standard of living for many families."*

This policy was consistent with Indian government approaches which provide for affirmative action on behalf of disadvantaged groups such as scheduled castes and tribes.

The PO, ITDA (Paderu) holds the office of Honorary President of AASSAV by virtue of his office. The activities of the Society are carried out in close cooperation with this office and with other government departments such as the District Rural Development Association (DRDA) in Visakhapatnam and Tribal Welfare in Hyderabad (the head office for tribal development). One of AASSAV's goals was to bridge between outside agencies and local communities in the effective implementation of development programmes.

The benefits in establishing a totally Adivasi organisation were firstly, the members share the same language and culture as the target groups of literacy and development programmes. Interaction in this way is always more productive than across language and cultural divides. Secondly, Adivasi staff all grew up in these communities and live permanently in these localities. The bond between AASSAV and the people they serve is close and constant and, unlike government agencies and NGOs run by non-tribals, they will not be moved on to another project or agency. This ensures continuity and accountability towards the beneficiaries of the programmes and projects.

CIDA agreed to fund the newly formed society on a three-yearly basis. By the end of three years, it was intended that the profit from the income generating activities (IGAs) could be used to support the literacy programmes. Until that time, CIDA's funding would be available to establish the Society which suggested that *"the main purpose ... is to further adult literacy and education and to integrate this with other development activities."* (Final Report 1990:9) The new team began to look at projects which would make income for them.

The rest of this chapter looks at the processes which AASSAV went through; the activities they pursued and the changes which occurred over the years.

The growth of the Society

Up to this point, all the work had taken place in an office in the village of Hattaguda. But now, a great deal of construction was being planned for the various projects that were intended. Activity in the early days was hectic and staffing rapidly increased as the organisation expanded and people with the appropriate skills were employed.

Land acquisition

For the headquarters, the team negotiated for a piece of land close to the village. It was an area full of rocks, stones and hard brown earth, but with extension possibilities. Agreement to sell was relatively easily achieved because all the land would be registered in the society's name and since the society was tribal, the land would not actually be leaving tribal control. Furthermore, AASSAV leaders, knowing the significance of land to the tribal people, made the decision that any family selling a piece of land to AASSAV would automatically be eligible for one family member's full time employment with AASSAV. In this way the family would maintain its connection to ancestral lands, and not lose potential income.

The Project Officer at ITDA wanted AASSAV also to purchase land on the edge of Araku Valley as he had it in mind to develop tourism. Plans were made for building and people were sent for training in hotel management in Visakhapatnam. The plans for the hotel, however, did not materialise, as the bank would not provide a loan. There were also plans for a petrol station in the same locality and another piece of land was bought for this, but once again this did not materialise as the contract was given to someone else. While the negotiations were going on, first vegetables and then trees were planted on these sites and it was out of this initiative of the AASSAV leadership that the idea for coffee plantations began to develop. These plantations would perform several functions: demonstration, employment, income generation and environmental improvement. The team decided to buy only waste or semi-waste land for the development of coffee plantations and more and more land was added until they had 26 acres at the headquarters alone.

Because of the condition of the purchased land pick axes and crowbars had to be used to break open the soil and carry out the rocks. Hundreds of people worked to clear the land. Many of the walls now seen around the land were made with the cleared rocks. Before the coffee plantations were established, vegetables were grown and sold at the markets.

After people saw the possibilities for land improvement, some even came to AASSAV with proposals to sell land. A dairy farm, for example, was established on land that had not been used within living memory. The land in question was close to the town so it was valuable and developers wanted it. The owners really wanted to keep it, but on hearing what AASSAV was doing, requested that the Society buy the 40 acres. In this way, they could still keep their connection to it. In fact the family to whom the land originally belonged are still working on it.

Construction of the Headquarters

The first building was planned as a print shop. Books were being produced for the literacy programme and every time they needed a print run the work had to be sent to Visakhapatnam, or Chennai, which was very expensive. The AASSAV team decided that they should do their own printing. With the help of a visiting architect they came up with a plan and in 1989 a print shop was opened with a treadle press machine. A group of trainees was sent to Chennai for 18 months to gain the necessary training and experience in printing. Others were sent for accounting and typing training in Visakhapatnam.

Funding

John Cairns, CIDA's evaluator who, together with CIDA had recommended change, had always strongly endorsed the AASSAV project and at each evaluation recommended that CIDA continue its financial support. Three times funding had been provided for 3 years until in 1996 when it was decided that this should be the final 3-year funding phase after which AASSAV should have been financially independent. But after approval for new funds had been given, an unforeseen problem arose. AASSAV discovered that they had been wrongly informed by the bank manager of SBI that they did not require special registration to receive foreign funds. Now they found out that every organisation receiving foreign funds was required by the Government of India to register with the Foreign Contributions office in Delhi. AASAAV needed to complete this registration before it could receive any further funds from CIDA and LEAD.

With the help of various contacts, such as the District Collector and the Commissioner of Tribal Welfare, the case for AASSAV was made. Two AASSAV staff and a colleague from Visakhapatnam went to New Delhi with a letter of introduction to the Foreign Contributions Registration office. Because of the novelty of visiting Adivasis from Andhra Pradesh, and in spite of the high security, they were ushered straight through. The official, amazed that tribal people could discuss their project with him, was very kind to them. The Collector's letter, together with a letter from the project officer, helped immensely in what would otherwise have been a very difficult process. Even so, the registration took 18 months to be approved and by that time the projects AASSAV had started suffered great damage. Some programmes had to be stopped, many animals died and many of the well-trained staff left.

The remainder of the chapter looks at the scope of the projects initiated by AASSAV and the challenges faced in their implementation and sustainability. It begins here with a discussion on the nature and history of "projects" and the ways in which aid and development operate.

The nature of projects

Governments, NGOs and donor agencies have generally relied on implementing individual, well-defined projects as a way of generating development. Most use a logical framework analysis to put in order pre-defined sets of objectives, assumptions, activities and resources, resulting in measurable benefits and impacts within certain time constraints (Fowler 1997:17). This way of "doing development" has rarely been sustainable because it has usually been imposed by outsiders, lacking the essential long term support and has not been rooted in local social customs and ideologies. More recently, development experts have realised the limitations of projects which are not part of holistic development rooted in the empowerment of communities and now recommend participatory approaches as a necessary prerequisite for sustainable development. However, development work has rarely been given time to become an established part of the way of life of the communities, because donors and governments seldom want to fund over long periods. The State Director of CARE India suggested another problem, arguing that:

"...social change is fundamental and a prerequisite for bringing about sustainable development impact. Therefore, any programme that intends to make sustainable development impact needs to implement appropriate strategies to bring about sustainable social change. People external to the community by themselves cannot bring about social change. Only the target community can do so. This means that the programme planned should provide enough time for community organisation and conscientisation processes and offer support to the communities' choice of interventions." K.Gopalan, State Director, CARE – STEP, AP (Brochure 2003)

"Projects" continue to be used, however, chiefly because they are well suited to Western bureaucratic aid systems. Although the focus changed to tailoring the intervention to local circumstances, with greater efforts to involve the beneficiaries, there continued to be many difficulties experienced by the recipients of development projects. These common occurrences suggested by Fowler (2001) were also experienced by AASSAV. For example:

- Promised financial time frames were often changed by the donor keeping AASSAV in a state of insecurity. The amount of information mandated by the donor before disbursement of funds often increased and the computerisation of the surveys, which was also a requirement, slowed the process.

- Projects were terminated and promises of development work or finances did not materialised, without consideration for the beneficiaries or for AASSAV.

- The consequences of some projects have had unintended effects, such as creating more work for the women and so the innovations are not used.

- In some cases, success has been equated with provision of materials rather than its usefulness to the recipients.

■ Accountability has been equated with accounting of financial or material resources rather than whether development has actually taken place and the projects have achieved their aims.

The focus of development more recently changed towards participatory empowerment programmes, which may eliminate some of the problems noted above, but in all cases, genuine participation is difficult, takes time, and requires trust between the agencies. This means a release of some of the control by the development agency or donor of planning, implementation and results. Donors and development agencies find themselves frustrated and impatient which is often a result of not truly understanding and appreciating the consequences of sharing the control, or the difficulties faced by those in remote often pre-literate societies. While some of the partners preferred to bypass AASSAV and "do the work" themselves rather than build AASSAV's capacity, CIDA was always very sympathetic. However, little guidance was provided to AASSAV, who were new to this type of work.

When AASSAV was first established, then, the main focus was to initiate development through projects and the expectation was that the organisation would become self-financing so that literacy programmes could be maintained. At the end of that first funding period, however, it was noted by Cairns (Evaluation Report 1990:30) that while many literacy projects in developing countries have reached self-management, very few had been able to achieve financial self-sufficiency. So would AASSAV be able to do what few other development organisations had done and become independent and if so, how would this status be achieved?

Projects of AASSAV

In 1988 there were no development projects, except literacy and, as stated above, income-generating projects were set up to make a profit *"to support an ongoing adult literacy and education programme"* (Evaluation Report 1987). No predefined programmes were stipulated by either CIDA or LEAD and ideas of how to generate income were discussed in the executive committee.

For the AASSAV team and for the Coordinator, development work was a new and difficult challenge. The change from social work to the business of project management was an enormous step and new skills, not found in indigenous cultures, such as accounting and reporting within a time frame, had to be learned. And indeed the AASSAV team did develop technical skills as well as a capacity to organise and manage projects.

Of the various projects implemented some were successful while others were not. The projects were intended to be models which local people could take up later on their own. And it was further intended that each project implemented should make enough money to pay back the loan which started it, as well as feed back into AASSAV's education work.

As a registered NGO, AASSAV could work with state and local government development agencies implementing and managing programmes and projects on their behalf. At times AASSAV had to put more finances into the projects than was intended as costs often overreached the amounts the government provided. On occasion, the government did not pay the originally agreed amount and reimbursement was invariably late. Nonetheless, although these projects did not necessarily generate income for AASSAV, they kept AASSAV members employed, covered some of the overheads and staff salaries, and provided training and experience.

In the late 1980s when AASSAV was the only NGO in the area, and India still had not liberalized its economy, the goods and services readily available today were not so then. AASSAV had no telephone for the first twelve years and the print shop was the only one in the area and the ITDA and local businesses gave AASSAV contracts. At that time, it was hard to attract the support needed to build AASSAV's capacity, but much changed with economic liberalisation which happened in the early 1990s. The impact was felt in Araku Valley as private shops were opened; materials became available which had never been seen in the interior and access to the plains now became much easier. For AASSAV the results of liberalisation were both positive and negative; it was impossible for AASSAV to compete with the larger printing companies, but with better communication and local availability of education and entertainment, people from the plains no longer minded staying in Araku Township.

Development projects for self-sufficiency

Within the first funding period of three years from 1987 to 1990, the new Society operated three registered businesses and a total of eight income-generating projects. These included the print shop, stationery and book sales, vegetable and fruit farms, a sheep farm, a rabbit farm, beekeeping, carpentry and social forestry. Many seemed good ideas in the beginning, and although some succeeded, others, for one reason or another, ceased to operate as they failed to cover the costs of operation, let alone make money for the organisation.

Training personnel

In order to begin the income generating activities and to manage the headquarters, there was a need to train people in many different aspects of the work including accounting and book-keeping, typing, driving and mechanics, in reporting and corresponding in English, in translation of written materials for publication, as well as in the use of printing machines.   At the start, there were no trained and no full time staff, but by 1990 there were over one hundred employees.

Training courses were in
- **The management of small scale industries:** two men.

- **Driving:** Four drivers were sent for training, two of whom were too afraid to continue.   One other who already had a licence was hired and sent to develop his driving skills.

- **Typing:** Three typists were trained in the city in government recognised institutes.   The trainees sent for bookkeeping also learned typing.

- **Printing:** Five trainees were sent to Chennai for 18 months for print shop training, others were trained on the job in the new print shop. Two more were trained in ruling and binding, both in Visakhapatnam and by visiting trainers.

- **Hotel Management:** In the early stages of the Society, it had been suggested that AASSAV should be involved in the tourist trade. With this in mind, nine young men were sent to Visakhapatnam for in-service training at the Food Craft Institute and good hotels in the city.   This was not at all successful for a number of reasons: firstly, the tribal men faced high competition; secondly, their English was not adequate, thirdly, they were not treated well in the city and fourthly, there were times the tribal men did not attend work because there was some family or community commitment (which always comes first).

- **Carpentry:** Two carpenters were trained in the city and when construction began at the new Headquarters, they were recalled and worked alongside experienced carpenters. Others were trained later on the job as the work load increased.

- **Electrician:** One young man who had trained on a government training course as an electrician, was hired and sent for more training.   He, too, was recalled when the building work started and became   the   manager   of   the   Construction   and   Maintenance

Department. Others were then trained under him.

The rule was to send at least two people on any training and this proved valuable to the organisation as many who had been trained were later lost to government jobs (see Chapter 4: Management).

Income Generating Projects

The following section looks at the beginnings and progress of the various projects AASSAV implemented.

The Print Shop

The print shop was opened in 1989 with two sections: the English-Adivasi Oriya section and the Telugu-Adivasi Oriya section. More up to date printing machines were purchased as the need arose, the latest, a desktop publishing unit and a larger offset machine, being bought in 2002.

The high costs of printing the literacy materials in Visakhapatnam or Chennai made the print shop invaluable to the literacy programme. And when the print shop was first established AASSAV was given government orders, mainly from ITDA. Even though there are often large, simple printing jobs required by government departments within the Agency Area, they are no longer given to AASSAV. They orders go out to tender and AASSAV cannot compete with the larger companies. The distance of the print shop from businesses prevented some from giving orders to AASSAV and the erratic nature of the supply of electricity and the high costs of using the generator meant that profits were reduced. The AASSAV print shop could have provided employment and income for tribal youths, and if would have been nice if ITDA again supported this tribal society by providing work. This way the print shop could be sustainable, but it has never been used to its fullest capacity.

When the print shop was built, a warehouse for the Stationery and Book Sales was also constructed. Sales first began with village outlets to support the literacy efforts of both the Society and the Government. Four shops were opened and although business was good at first, private owners soon opened stationery shops in the township and sales were reduced. The salaries had to be covered and when no profit was made the shops had to be closed; one in 2001 and two more in 2003.

Carpentry

The carpentry shop was set up to support the work of AASSAV at headquarters and the projects generally. Buildings, fencing and so on were necessary to AASSAV's projects. There was discussion about how this could also be used for income generation, but until 2003 progress was slow since the government had not yet authorized the carpentry shop as a business; orders came mainly from AASSAV members. More orders were taken in 2003 and acacia wood from one plantation was used for making tables, chairs, beds and other items. Even so, little money was made.

Sewing and Handicraft Centre
The government asked AASSAV to train young women in sewing and so when the training began a Sewing and Handicrafts Centre was set up as an income generating project. Each training course, funded by IFAD and ITDA, lasted for one year and included sewing and handicrafts along with literacy, agriculture and animal husbandry. The programmes were very positive and altogether lasted for five years, after which the funds were discontinued and the programme and the centre were closed. It never became a source of profit for AASSAV.

Transport
AASSAV purchased a truck at a time when no transport was available locally. It was used for transportation in AASSAV's project work and also for transporting the farmers' vegetable crops to Visakhapatnam's farmers' markets. The business was closed when it began to lose money through the difficulties of management. However, the driver then bought his own truck through an ITDA project and continues to transport goods as a private business.

Restaurant
It had been planned to have a tea and coffee shop in the grounds of the MACS (Mutually Aided Cooperative Society) Bank[2] so that AASSAV coffee from its plantations and milk and milk products from the dairy farm could be used and sold. A garden was planted and shelters put up, but without proper consultation the original plans were changed and the shop itself was built on the road in front of the bank. This was operated for a short time, but it soon became clear that without adequate supervision it would not be successful and it was rented out to a local hotel owner who runs it as a "fast food" restaurant.

Rice and Flour Mill
The mill operated successfully for a number of years and local people were very glad to have one in the locality. Without it the women

---

[2] See page 57.

would have to walk the 5 or more kilometres into Araku Valley township to mill their rice and grain which cost time, money and energy. However, the number of staff manning the mill meant that it could not cover its overheads. The mill was closed in 2004 and the machinery was bought by two members of AASSAV who relocated it to a new milling house in the village. The local people were eager for it to start operating again and it is now a busy private mill.

Land Based Activities

Land has always been important in tribal life. Many groups operated a system of shifting cultivation, known as podu cultivation, relying at the same time on forest products for their livelihoods. Podu cultivation leads to soil impoverishment and erosion and has now been outlawed. And with the forest either disappearing or protected, this livelihood is in decline. Now many are working as agricultural day labourers and eking out a meagre living from the forest produce. Land based activities were therefore seen as a possible source of income for AASSAV and have turned out to be an important aspect of AASSAV's influence and experience. However, the land based activities began incidentally.

While waiting for permission to build the hotel and petrol station, the land was used for growing vegetables and then, when the projects did not materialise, beginning in the 1990s, silver oak trees were planted in preparation for coffee plantations.

Vegetable, flower and fruit farm

Where water, compost and fertiliser are available, conditions are extremely favourable for growth in the Araku Valley so when AASSAV began the cultivation of vegetables, flowers and fruit they expected good results. However there were several difficulties and drawbacks with the vegetable growing. The soils were not always good as much had been eroded and leached. A lot of fertilizer had to be used which costs money, reducing profits. The tribal people were inexperienced in field work and much had to be taught. Sometimes they did not water, because the way they had grown things in the past was rain dependent. They had to learn that no water meant no crops. Seeds and seed supply were often unreliable.

While some of the problems were contained, others remained a problem. Fields were levelled, soil erosion check dams made, trees planted for shade and wind breaks and much fertilizer was used. Obtaining good seed, however, was always difficult as was the marketing of the produce. Marketing was not something they had learned to do at that time, but as they did not get good prices from wholesalers, a shop was opened in the township. This did well for a time, but family farms do not count the cost of labour and so income is generated, but as a business it did not pay.

At one time, the government introduced a new crop - potatoes. Extension workers taught the farmers how to grow and look after the crop and for the first year things went well. The next year the seed potato came too late. Another year the harvested potatoes were kept in storage and the government never came to collect them as they had promised - the people had sacks of potatoes rotting in their homes. When the government officials arrived the year after, the farmers, not surprisingly, refused to work on the project. AASSAV was even asked to help, but this made no difference. Then the farmers decided that now they knew how to grow vegetables, including potatoes, they would do so themselves. They formed a cooperative, bought the seed and when the harvest came in they hired a truck and took the vegetables down to the markets in Visakhapatnam themselves. Since then, every Friday a truck has travelled down the mountains to the Farmers' Market in the city.

Even with all the expenditures of going to Visakhapatnam, there were improved financial gains. In the local markets, where wholesalers come to buy they would get only 3 rupees a kilo, and many times they were cheated. The wholesalers say they are not interested and the people wait in the heat beside the road until the afternoon and as they do not want to return home with their loads and many of these vegetables would spoil, they either have to sell at a low price or throw the produce away. They prefer to go to the farmers' markets where they can get at least 8 rupees per kilo and they know they are not being cheated. Sometimes they make money and sometimes they do not, but it is satisfying to have been in control of the process themselves. There is a sense of achievement in doing business without being cheated.

There were some disasters with the crops. In tomato growing, for example, sticks were never used to hold the plants up: the plants were left lying on the ground. Some rotted and were eaten by animals so they tried growing with sticks. This time they had wonderful tomatoes, but then nematodes destroyed the plants. Experts from the Agricultural University of Hyderabad, Chintapalli Extension Unit, were called in to help, but nothing could be done, so they stopped growing tomatoes.

AASSAV itself no longer grows vegetables as the returns are not sufficient to cover the costs of the labour, but many families continue to use what they have learned if they have their land available.

Coffee plantations

The first coffee plantations were established on land which, as mentioned earlier, had been purchased for other purposes; a hotel and a fuel station. When the contracts were given elsewhere AASSAV turned the land over to trees or vegetables and later to coffee. Shade trees were planted the first year and once these were established, coffee was planted, usually after two or three years. Shade trees were mainly silver oak, as they are fast growing and easy to maintain on waste land, but among them were planted wild palm trees, palm oil trees, trees that have a seed for natural dyeing, jackfruit, guava, banana, mango, mulberry and pine trees, which are excellent for carpentry. Pepper vines, initially obtained from the government, were grown up the trunks of silver oak. The produce from the trees in the plantations was used, or sold, as appropriate.

For two years irrigation had to be available, but when the crop matured, rain was generally sufficient to feed the plants. Some plantations had no water and no electricity and for the first year the women who cared for the new plants had to water them by hand; an ideal model for local farmers as many of them have no access to irrigation water and would also have to water by hand.

The first AASSAV coffee was planted in 1993 and by 2003 fifty acres of coffee in five plantations were being cared for by AASSAV. Most of the land bought for coffee was waste hillside land, rocky and arid, but after five years, the reclaimed land looked as if forest had always grown there. The coffee plantations proved to be a success not only in growing coffee but in land reclamation as well.

Sericulture

Each plantation had its own characteristics, each with a story different from the others. For example, on one plantation, following a government programme, mulberry trees were grown for silkworm culture. One year when the time came to harvest the silk, the silkworms died of disease. This was the initial cause of the project's abandonment, but there were other problems: it was labour intensive, the market was unreliable and climatic conditions were not conducive to sericulture. Only the government purchased cocoons and AASSAV staff had to deliver them to Paderu (50kms away) as well as pick up the seed from there. For all these reasons the project was not financially viable and sericulture was never restarted.

Family Coffee Farmers Project

In 1998, AASSAV was asked to work on the Integrated Coffee Development Programme for ITDA. 1,407 families in 80 villages were assigned to AASSAV, which managed and supervised the preparation of the land for the coffee plants for all the participating families. Most farmers had one acre or less on infertile, rocky, hillside land, which would not reap much of a crop in any year and if the monsoon rains were weak there would be none at all. AASSAV provided all coffee saplings (12,00,000) from the nursery at the headquarters and supervised secondary nurseries in interior places. Nursery planting began in February 1999 and after 45 days the seedlings were taken to the secondary nurseries in central interior villages with enough plants for up to eight villages in each.

AASSAV already had the personnel available through the literacy programme to provide supervisors who lived in or near the localities. For government officials, data collection in the tribal region had always been difficult as officers were asked to cover large areas without vehicles and with little understanding of the local language and culture. Little could be achieved in terms of supervision under these conditions. AASSAV's supervisors were local people who lived in the villages and who had been trained to keep good records for reporting back to headquarters. With the president's and the coordinator's help, they were able to fulfil government reporting demands.

The plans with ITDA were made, the Coffee Board of India was to provide technical assistance and a Coffee Growers Association was to be established. There were also plans for literacy centres in the 80 villages for the participating families as well as for other members of the villages. The newsletter was to be revived to disseminate information on coffee cultivation, with articles which would also benefit other Self Help Groups (SHGs). There was to be a revolving fund, which would help the coffee growers through their first seven years after which the plantations would be financially self-sustaining. But then, after the silver oak was planted in 1995, and the coffee was planted in 1999 (a year later), ITDA withdrew. The 1407 farmers were left on their own without the help and support they needed to improve their farming skills and to develop their crops so that good fruit was produced. There was no financial support, no help with fertilizer requirements, and no help with training in the care of the plants; nor was there any help in marketing the coffee. Because fences were not built, animals came in and destroyed the young trees, or people cut them for sticks, or they died from lack of water or some other reason. Some farmers looked after their plants, but others did not have the knowledge, or the funds to care for them. In spite of such odds stacked against them, about 1000 farmers out of the 1407 had maintained the coffee sufficiently to continue with coffee farming. But support was essential if these farms were to be sustainable. This support eventually came from a funding agency based in Hyderabad.

The Naandi Foundation was set up by four major corporations based in Hyderabad who wanted to support the development of Andhra Pradesh. Naandi had found out about the work of AASSAV from another NGO working in the area and first approached AASSAV in 2000. Throughout 2000-2001 AASSAV was in consultation with Naandi to draw up an agreement between them to support the coffee farmers. The coordinator, the president and other members of staff spent many hours preparing a Logical Framework Analysis to present an acceptable proposal to Naandi. Visits between Hyderabad and AASSAV were frequent and many changes were made to the proposal before an agreement was reached.

It was estimated that seven years input was required before the farmers would be able to repay their loans and obtain a good income for the family. Anything less would be unreliable for local development. In early discussions with Naandi it had been agreed to fund for seven years, but modifications were made in the funding period as well as in the amounts. The time was reduced to three and finally, to one year at a time with the option of withdrawing after a 6-monthly review. CIDA and LEAD had committed to a three year period of funding for AASSAV's involvement in the Farmers' Coffee Project. While project reviews are always needed and changes may be appropriate, if no long term commitment is made by the donor, it is the farmer who bears the weight of insecurity and risk.

The project was originally intended to start in November 2001, which was essential if plants were to be saved, but there were many delays. For example, when AASSAV drew up a survey as part of the preparatory phase to find exact numbers and details of all the families involved, more information was required by Naandi and an extended survey was formulated. The new survey covered the state of the plantations, the progress of the farming and the impact of the project so that the farmers' economic and social improvements could be monitored. The data was put into a specially designed computer programme supplied by Naandi. It took time to rewrite the survey, it took more time than expected to conduct the extended survey and it took longer than anticipated to transfer the data to the computer.

The AASSAV head office needed support to develop appropriate accounting facilities. Three people were sent to AASSAV by Naandi for two days to work with the accounting and other computer systems to make sure things were soundly in place for the disbursement of funds and accounting, as well as for the recovery of bank loans which the new farmers' groups would be involved in.

On 9 March 2002, it was announced that the project had officially started. The training and the computer programmes had not been installed by then, but it was felt that sufficient had been done by AASSAV to receive the funds for disbursement. However, the funds were not released: Naandi stated that they were still not satisfied and asked for CIDA funds to be used for the initial stages of the project. Changes in the starting date caused problems for the farmers in applying fertiliser and building protective fencing, but eventually the essential work was completed.

Naandi established an office at AASSAV headquarters with two Naandi officers in charge and from this office all the operations for the coffee project take place. Initially, there was some collaboration between Naandi and AASSAV, but for the most part, Naandi controlled the coffee project, using AASSAV members as supervisors.

The coffee farmers living in the eighty villages were spread across two mandals. This was divided into ten zones or clusters with one hundred farmers in each group. Each group elected a president and secretary and AASSAV provided one supervisor for each zone. This was increased in 2003 to seventeen with the extra supervisors assigned where the needs arose. Most of the supervisors had also been involved in the literacy programme; they lived in the area and knew the people well.

The farmers from each village formed a cooperative for savings and loans and opened accounts with the AASSAV Cooperative (MACS) Bank. The many pressing needs among the farmers mean that there is no guarantee that money given as cash will be used for the right purpose so the disbursement of funds would come only after work had been completed. AASSAV, in conjunction with the MACS bank, provided loans to the farmers to pay for labour for building walls and fences. The bio-fertilizer was given, but very carefully supervised and monitored to ensure it was actually used and not sold. Naandi brought in a specialist from Mumbai to train supervisors and farmers in making their own bio-fertilizer. Thirty bins for organic fertilizer had already been built in 2003 on AASSAV's Dairy Farm, which would be used for AASSAV's own plantations and be sold where there was excess. The coffee farmers would make their own.

The quality of the coffee improves with age, and at about 10 years, if the plant has been well cared for, the coffee matures and thus a better price can be obtained, depending, of course, on global market prices. Because AASSAV had had experience with marketing their own coffee, it was agreed that it should market the coffee for the farmers so that they would not have to rely on wholesalers. AASSAV's capacity for processes of pulping and drying were increased to cater for 1000 farmers. After the berries are harvested, they are packed, weighed and recorded for each plantation day by day. When the coffee is dried, the number of kilos of dried beans harvested from each plantation can be calculated. Labour inputs, amounts of fertilizer required and profits from each plantation can be calculated. This information is essential if operations are to be efficient.[3]

The coffee farmers Federation was formed and they were encouraged to join the Coffee Board Association. Each group chose one man as their representative; someone who could read and write so that when they visited the coffee growers' office they could understand the records.

AASSAV insisted on having the farmers' coffee plantations operating in organic mode from the beginning. This was approved by Naandi and organic certification was obtained. Since organic buyers prefer to buy direct from the producers Naandi worked on branding and professional packaging. In 2005, the harvest was good and already making money for the farmers. The 2005 crop was sold as organic coffee through Naandi with an international tie-up for which the farmers received a very good income. Part of the profit was put back into the Federation to improve their long term sustainability.

This was AASSAV's first experience of relating closely with a partner organisation and the process was a steep learning curve for both organisations. There were areas of disagreement between Naandi and AASSAV on what should be included in the project, such as literacy classes, the number of supervisors for each area and the need for good quality meals and cultural programmes during training

---

[3] Other benefits from the coffee plantations include black pepper, the harvest of Silver Oak for paper mills, fruit and some vegetables or spices.

sessions. Compromises have to be made on both sides at times for positive partnerships to develop; so while Naandi conceded to the inclusion of literacy, they did not agree to fund two supervisors, nor would they provide extra funds for good meals at training programmes. Where possible and appropriate, AASSAV has attempted to find funds to supply what they perceived to be essential components in the project.

There is no doubt that AASSAV, nor the farmers, by themselves, could have never provided the professional input necessary to achieve such high quality production and marketing of organic coffee. The Naandi team has made remarkable progress in the Farmers' Coffee Project, but the concern expressed by the coordinator is that it become a Naandi project and in the process AASSAV has been marginalised. The relationship between AASSAV, a tribal organisation, and Naandi, an efficient, sophisticated urban business with highly qualified personnel is described in more detail in Chapter 5.

Animal Husbandry

The Animal Husbandry projects were started as income generating projects for AASSAV, but with a view to encouraging local community development through some of these, such as the dairy farms. However, each one suffered greatly during the funding interruptions in 1994 and again in 1997-98. For such businesses to become self-sustaining there needs to be continuous funding as well as professional input; the lack of these were partly responsible for the failure of these projects.

The Sheep Farm

Raising sheep was one of the first of AASSAV's projects. The people knew how to look after sheep and the local market could handle meat products at a good price. Over time, however, AASSAV learned that sustaining the project would require a minimum of 200 breeding females. Funds were not available to purchase the initial stock as well as the number of rams required. When the delay in the funds occurred in 1998, AASSAV sold the sheep and the project was closed.

Bees and Honey

At the headquarters there are 20-30 beehives maintained by two men. They are able to collect the honey from November onwards for several months during the flowering season. The honey is of high quality and is sold locally. Training in beekeeping was provided when government programmes required it. The carpentry shop makes the hives either for local use or for those who have been trained. This is a low cost project and has continued to operate.

Rabbits

Tribal people used to hunt rabbits and other game, but with little game left and therefore less protein in their diet, the health of the tribal people had deteriorated. Families often do not have the money to buy meat, but a small rabbit farm with a hutch would be possible. Rabbits would provide meat for the family and for sale to neighbours and in the market. AASSAV discussed the project with those concerned, area representatives were chosen, rabbit cages were made, training took place, and some even started growing grass. With 1000 rabbits at headquarters, they were ready to provide the families with rabbits.

Then during the financial crisis of 1998 AASSAV had no funds to buy feed necessary for the 1000 breeding mothers. Females began to kill their babies as they didn't have enough milk and when this started to happen, AASSAV decided to close down and sell them immediately and the project was given up.

It was decided, when the funding eventually arrived, that this project would not be started up again as it was too costly. The barn was used for the coffee project.

Chickens

Raising chickens seemed like a good idea. Chicken is a popular food in the area and the local market seemed able to absorb any number of chickens. The chicks were brought from Visakhapatnam and although the chickens produced were of good quality, the project did not make money. Firstly, expensive feed was required and secondly, if too many chickens reached the optimum weight at the same time, it was not possible to sell them all at once. Having to feed them beyond this optimum weight increased expenses to the point that when they were eventually sold, it was at a loss.

The solution was to turn to a local variety of chicken that can eat husks and waste instead of the highly concentrated feed. The women's groups could have small free range, organic chicken farms, using a special breed of chicken called 'Mountain Chicken'. This idea was never followed through after the funding problem.

The Dairy Farm

The dairy farm, started in May 1995 as a model farm, is situated on 35 acres of land that had not been used in living memory. The land was planted with trees and fodder crops. The dairy farm was started with a Friesian Holstein breed of milking cows crossed with Indian breeds so that they can withstand the climate. Two milk men and a manager went on a government training course with ITDA for one month, learning how to feed, clean and milk.

At the same time four families with land for farming were to be provided with cows for a pilot project of Family Dairy Farms. Husbands and wives together had come to the AASSAV headquarters for training and the land had been planted with trees and prepared for fodder crops. These families were all located near to government administrative centres so that they could walk everyday to the centre with the milk produce.

In the beginning the milk being produced was sufficient, but the farm was badly affected by the 1997-1998 funding problem. They were not able to buy the feed required, nor plant the fodder; as a result of which they had almost no feed at all and the cows stopped giving milk. The fodder they had dried out and died because, although there was river water available, there was no fuel and no parts for the irrigation pumps. Fifteen animals died: a devastating loss.

In 2001 there were 16 cows left, 7 of which were calves. Buying feed from the plains and transporting it to Araku was too expensive, and the milk produced did not cover the costs, so the cows were taken down to the plains to be sold. By 2002 there was only one cow and its calf left. In September 2003, four good breed milk-producing buffalo were purchased in the hope and expectation that these would be more suitable to the region. A young tribal man with a science degree was hired and trained as farm manager.

The wisdom of continuing with the dairy farm is still in question, and the family dairy farms were never restarted, but the farm is being used for other purposes as well. A large production unit for vermiculture was built and the bio-fertiliser produced was entirely from farm produce - weeds, banana trees (after the fruit) and manure - this was used on the coffee plantations.

Government Programmes

The Girls' Training Programme

The Vanitha Girls' training programme, originally introduced in 1994, was intended for girl dropouts between the ages of 12 and 14 years. It was a 12 month programme which provided a range of skills and handicraft training including horticulture, social forestry, animal husbandry, health, hygiene and nutrition as well as sewing and knitting. Besides this the girls went through the Adivasi Oriya –

Telugu literacy programme. It was initially funded by the International Fund for Agricultural Development (IFAD), later supported by the ITDA and run by AASSAV. It ran for six years until the funds at ITDA ran out. ITDA wanted AASSAV to run a large hostel (for up to 300 girls) so that the girls could come in from a greater distance, but AASSAV were reluctant to do this; the girls are very difficult to control.

From 1994 to 2000, 214 girls had been enrolled in the course, all from villages within 5 kilometers distance so they could walk in every day and return at night. Most of the girls graduated; a very high completion rate. One important effect of this programme was that it demonstrated that girl dropouts have the capacity to learn to read and write and acquire a variety of skills. It became so popular that parents from distant villages made requests to AASSAV for their daughters to be enrolled.

Attitudes towards girls and women in the community are beginning to change; more girls are being educated, and more women are being respected for their ability to earn. Many of the girls who went through this training are now married and taking part in the women's self-help groups.

Bio-gas ovens
This was a government initiated programme through the renewable energy department in conjunction with a university. It was a "good idea" and with proper teaching, training and follow-up, it could have worked. It had been worked out that bio-gas could be made from the manure of two cows and so the ovens were given to families with two buffalo or cows. The problem was that the idea had been tested in the plains where cows are bigger and produce more waste. In the hills it would have taken at least four animals to provide sufficient manure to make gas. About 200 ovens were installed, none of which is currently operating. Besides the problem of insufficient manure, the oven created more work for the women who had to look after it. The women had to "feed" the bio-gas oven every day with dung which needed to be in liquid form. They also had to extract the slurry and make an arrangement for storage until it would be used. All this had not been considered and the workload which the women already have would not permit them to include this additional work. This was an example of top down implementation, which did not work. Maybe one day people will have enough economic power to own four cows and bio-gas ovens will be used in their homes.

MACS (Mutually Aided Cooperative Society) Bank

Poor farmers and small businesses are generally excluded from conventional financial institutions and have to resort to informal ways of saving, insuring and borrowing – usually from moneylenders at extortionate rates of interest. In the 1980s and 1990s, NGOs began savings and credit groups following the lead of the Grameen Bank in Bangladesh. At the same time, non-land based activities were introduced to reduce poverty, and poor landless people were being targeted.

AASSAV was approached by DRDA to run a cooperative bank for Araku Valley Mandal, but from the beginning there were difficulties. Getting the promised funding from the government to convert the building was problematic and left AASSAV with a large bill. It was promised that the women's groups banking with other banks would be transferred to the MACS bank, but that never materialized. The AASSAV staff needed good training and although arrangements were made with other banks in the area, the training scheme was limited and not really successful. Later AASSAV approached Naandi for help in organising and running the bank, and at first they were eager to do so and to include the coffee farmers in it, but for efficient management they needed to have full control. There was opposition to this from DRDA, who decided to take it back under their control. Several loans had been given unofficially to friends and AASSAV members, a move which could have had very serious repercussions. CARE then was asked for help in restructuring and operating the bank and using it for the new women's groups they were setting up under the STEP programme (see below). Finally, another government initiative, the Velugu project, focusing on women's development offered to help.

AASSAV has had a chequered history with the bank, much of it due to inexperience, lack of proper training and good supervision, but cultural practices and the social order also interfered with good banking practices. Naandi's hands were tied by the government taking the responsibility, and whether CARE or the Velugu project can support AASSAV in it, or whether it will be taken completely out of AASSAV's hands remains to be seen.

Despite all the problems, the women's self help groups served by the bank and in which the CARE STEP is fully involved are experiencing many positive benefits. The women maintain that they are stronger as a group than as individuals and instead of men making all the decisions, the women are also involved. The benefits have an effect on the whole family. Men control their drinking habits, they have more hope for the future, children are able to go to school and college, clothes can be bought, better food obtained.

Costs

Table 1 reveals the costs of all the operations at AASSAV through the years of CIDA's support. The overall total is in excess of 10 million Canadian dollars. AASSAV itself was established during phase two.

Some of AASSAV's critics have suggested that the funds could have been utilised in a more constructive way, establishing AASSAV as a self sustaining organisation. While some of the criticisms have some truth, the tendency has been to disregard the difficulties AASSAV has faced in so many different areas, including devastating funding gaps when many projects were closed, and the loss of trained and experienced staff.

Income generation: Success or Failure?

AASSAV has tried a wide variety of projects – some succeeded, some failed and some evolved into forms that could succeed, for example through private enterprise. In all the experimentation the aim was to find projects that would be both sustainable and profitable in the local environment. It is easy in retrospect to observe which projects were more or less likely to succeed, given local conditions, but whatever the outcome of the projects valuable lessons were learned in the process. In terms of factors contributing to failure, AASSAV identified the erratic nature of the supply of funds, gaps occurring in 1994-95, in 1997-1998 and once more in 2000, as key problems. During these years all the projects were affected to some degree.

- The literacy programmes were stopped, some in the middle of a course, and only in 2003 were they restarted in partnership with Naandi – which lasted for one year.
- Without irrigation, yields from the coffee plantations and other farm produce decreased.
- The animal husbandry programmes suffered more than the others. There was no money to irrigate for fodder, and there was no money to buy feed. Many animals died, or had to be sold before they died.
- Many customers were lost during this time and the morale of the staff dropped drastically.
- There was no desire to work and many staff found outside work and left AASSAV.

Table 1
Financial support to literacy and development – 1984 to 2004

	Phase I Jan '84 – Dec '87	Phase II Jan '88 – Sept '90	Phase III Oct '90 – Dec '93	Phase IV Jan '94 – Jun '97	Phase V Jul '97 – Sept '00	Phase VI Jul '01 – Mar '04	Total	%
Operations								
Literacy & Administration	152,046	185,501	193,428	396,590	176,675	164,032	1,268,272	18.5
IGPs & Development			314,078	850,092	856,628	552,202	2,573,000	37.4
Collaborative Projects						349,364	349,364	5.1
Sub-Total	152,046	185,501	507,506	1,246,682	1,033,303	1,065,598	4,190,636	61.0
Capacity Building & Other								
Capacity Building	4,673	305,294	306,484	189,430	236,103	142,141	1,184,125	17.2
Other Expenses	27,504	21,122	80,714	133,528	122,347	103,572	488,787	7.1
Sub-Total	32,177	326,416	387,198	322,958	358,450	245,713	1,672,912	24.3
Canadian Staff & Admin								
Expatriate Staff	41,235	64,000	75,000	110,000	75,000	71,500	436,735	6.4
Canadian Administration	15,300	53,800	118,000	165,000	130,000	92,018	574,118	8.3
Sub-Total	56,535	117,800	193,000	275,000	205,000	163,518	1,010,853	14.7
Total	240,758	629,717	1,087,704	1,844,640	1,596,753	1,474,829	6,874,401	100.0
Literacy & Administration								
Staff	86,188	73,936	77,707	157,754	120,272	82,892	598,749	47.2
Materials & Operating	65,858	111,565	115,721	238,836	56,403	81,140	669,523	52.8
Expenses								
Total	152,046	185,501	193,428	396,590	176,675	164,032	1,268,272	100.0
IGPs & Development								
Staff			88,125	417,649	403,698	304,081	1,213,553	47.2
Materials & Operating			225,953	432,443	452,930	248,121	1,359,447	52.8
Expenses								
Total		0	314,078	850,092	856,628	552,202	2,573,000	100.0

Between 1988 when AASSAV was established and 2004, there was little or no funding for more than three of these years. Any "normal" business would have gone bankrupt during the first funding crisis. AASSAV has survived three such crises. One CIDA evaluator, however, suggested that although the gaps in external funding had a lot to do with the closure of many projects, there were other factors that weakened the effectiveness of these IGAs and contributed to their failure as sources of income. These included:

"weather conditions, market forces, lack of technical expertise and knowledge of business development, the size of AASSAV staff and unrealistic expectations for the income that would be generated." (Memo, 19.3.2001)

- Weather: the success of any agricultural project is dependent on the weather conditions as a matter of course, particularly in places where water for irrigation is a problem and the crop growth is dependent on rain – the rainfall in that same year (2000) was limited and the summer was hot and dry.

- Market forces: small income-generating projects often suffer when the local market is limited and the project itself is not large enough to break into the market dominated by the larger companies. In this case, the price of coffee was affected by worldwide supply and demand.

- Technical expertise: AASSAV had undertaken a wide range of projects including plantations, bee-keeping, sericulture, animal husbandry, tailoring and others. A wide range of expertise was required which was engaged from other sources such as government programmes, university agricultural extension programmes and the Coffee Board of India. Technical expertise within AASSAV itself needed to be developed for AASSAV to continue to expand and be successful.

- Understanding business: AASSAV did not have access to expertise in small business development. They had little or no advice in the choice of projects, or to help them assess or manage the business side, particularly the risk factors. Most projects were losing money. A financial management consultant was eventually contracted in 2001 and a business manager was hired in 2003.

Some have suggested that the way AASSAV was established with permanent members who had to be paid, was not an example of good business acumen. On the face of it this is true, but there were two reasons for this. Firstly, as an Adivasi NGO, AASSAV has always had high absenteeism due to the cultural constraints. Attendance was often very irregular. A survey of staff absenteeism found that on any given day 10% of staff were absent which made it extremely difficult to manage business operations. Most of the employees had other commitments: commitments to family and the necessities of the agricultural year - most have some land on which they and their families depend for food. Family and agricultural responsibilities always take priority. This meant that the Society needed to train at least two people for most positions if growth as a viable development NGO was to continue. Those with poor attendance were sometimes dismissed, although some leniency was required. It is difficult for tribal people to adopt a style of work that requires regular attendance and culturally inappropriate to dismiss staff unless for some misdemeanour. Besides this there was the promise of further projects with ActionAid, Care and Naandi. If staff had been dismissed, there would have been no-one to fill these positions, but the promised joint projects were often subject to long delays. Staff were re-assigned to the new projects which were beginning to gain momentum by 2003. These included the MACS bank, supervision of the Naandi coffee project and the CARE STEP Project. AASSAV had to train its own staff and always made it a practice to sponsor more than one trainee for any one activity in order to cover wastage and absenteeism. In the urban areas new staff can be hired at a day's notice, but in the Agency area this is not possible. Even now AASSAV suffers because there are not enough staff with sufficient education when required.

Secondly, because of the considerable unemployment in the vicinity, AASSAV had attempted to maintain everyone in employment. Many became members when they were hired for various projects; others were members because the family had sold land to them. As the labour needs decreased, the labour force was not reduced accordingly. The labour force required to clear the land and begin the work on the coffee plantations, for example, was far greater than the number required to maintain a mature plantation. The operating deficits were primarily the result of excessive staff costs. In order to minimize the problem of overstaffing, staff who left or retired were not replaced.

Although many staff were committed to AASSAV and were keen to work locally and for their own people, some inevitably looked for better paid work or government jobs which would give them financial and future security. AASSAV lost trained and educated staff to government jobs from 1994 and they were forced to hire others who again required training.

All AASSAV's income generating projects have been small scale with the exception of the coffee and black pepper. The high costs of transport has meant that they have access only to local markets. Inputs, too, have been high as supplies to maintain the IGAs have not been available locally (e.g. chicks and chicken feed). Other projects such as the print shop and carpentry existed in order to support the programme and only generated income incidentally. In hindsight it was unrealistic to expect the projects would be able to produce in excess of their running costs.

CARE STEP: a new way of working?

AASSAV experienced more changes in 2002 as they linked with the CARE STEP (Sustainable Tribal Empowerment Project). AASSAV's role was to assist in the implementation of "social development action for improving the quality of life and strengthening CBOs". For CARE this was a new style "project" which was being implemented not only in India, but also in sixteen other countries worldwide, funded by the European Commission. CARE was the coordinating NGO, working together with the government and local NGOs to mobilise, organise and empower village community groups to take responsibility for their own development. Current theory suggests that this is more likely to succeed than development projects imposed by government or NGO.

Many groups that were formed for various activities within the community do not operate successfully and it was the intention of the CARE programme to train the groups to encourage them to find their own solutions to the problems they themselves identify. The NGOs would help the community organisations access the services needed.

AASSAV was given responsibility for 259 villages in two mandal areas covering more than 10,000 households. Twelve full time members were appointed: one project coordinator, two mandal coordinators, eight community coordinators (CC) and one accountant. Each CC has to look after 25-30 villages with 1000-1300 families. Two hundred animators (community organisers), all of whom were local language speakers and from the villages, were trained by CARE to help strengthen the village committees by raising awareness of their roles and responsibilities, identifying problems, finding solutions and helping to access services. It was stated by CARE that AASSAV was the only NGO they were working with where all the animators were literate. Many of them had been through the original literacy programme or were children of those who had.

A field coordinator was appointed specifically to assist in developing AASSAV's capacity to deliver the programme. The first performance review carried out by CARE in July 2003 suggested that AASSAV needed capacity building in areas such as monitoring and evaluation, documentation and human resource development. The AASSAV staff were trained in Action Oriented Learning (AOL), in Participatory Rural Appraisal (PRA) and in Micro Level Planning (MLP). Regular meetings were conducted with the CBOs or the newly formed Community Action Groups (CAG) on capacity building and awareness raising so that the CAGs would be successful in accessing the resources they needed from the various sources available (DRDA, ITDA, MPDO. Forest Office, Primary Health, Education and other departments, and local NGOs).

A survey was conducted and plans formed for each village community. Programmes already being implemented were documented and this information was linked with information obtained from the ITDA. Discussions with and surveys of the communities determined what was most needed and with the full agreement of the community and in cooperation with the government plans were made to supply the need.

Because the tribal communities are marginalized and often ignored in development planning, this process was intended to enable them to see their own problems addressed. The project itself had few predetermined aims and objectives, although certain areas of development were suggested. The intention was to enable communities to access resources already available to the community through government and other agencies. The involvement of local NGOs with local community groups, together with government development agencies should lead to greater convergence in development efforts.

After one year in the field, the project found that apathy towards and pessimism about development programmes were prevalent among the tribal communities. Tribal people expected that immediate cash or material benefits would be forthcoming rather than having to embrace the more demanding process of experimenting with ideas and adapting strategies for overcoming problems, and they tended to be uninformed of ways of accessing their rights. However, as the programme progressed, and access to resources increased, many tribals saw the positive benefits of such training and motivation. For example, several villages stated that clean water was their main problem, women having to walk several kilometres every day to fetch water from a spring. In 2004, CARE helped the communities to access government funds to construct tanks close to the villages, piping the water in from the springs. Although CARE's Water engineers were sceptical at first, but with the help of AASSAV's president and supervisors the work was done entirely by the village communities and to both their own and CARE's satisfaction. The experience and ability of AASSAC was greatly beyond the expectation of CARE.

Conclusions

The changes in direction at AASSAV in its 18 year history have reflected changes in thought and direction in the wider development community. At the start it was intended that AASSAV should become self-financing in order that it might run projects with its own finances, particularly literacy. But even after 18 years AASSAV still has not achieved self-reliance, let alone run its own literacy projects. But few development organisations ever do attain full financial sustainability; all NGOs are dependent in some way on external funding. It seems unfair to censure AASSAV, a small tribal NGO, attempting to build local capacity and provide services on the front line, when international NGOs themselves maintain their operations on the basis of donations and grants, much of which comes from governments and the big donor agencies.

In its attempts to become self-supporting an unfortunate result was that literacy programmes actually suffered. Experienced members were needed to work on the management of income generating programmes and coupled with the lack of funds, the literacy programme to cease to operate altogether. In 1990 Cairns noted the problem:

> *"The focus on self-management and self-sufficiency has resulted in a lack of emphasis on literacy and adult education. Income generation, although an essential objective in itself, should provide support for the educational improvement of the tribal population. It will be counter-productive if, in the process of establishing well-managed income generating activities, the educational component is unduly sacrificed." (31)*

So, on the one hand AASSAV was invited to become self-supporting, while on the other it was criticised for being too inward looking and attempting to develop and support only itself and its members. In fact, attempts had been made through projects, such as the dairy farm, rabbits and chickens, as well as through government projects to support community development, but because AASSAV was given the target of becoming financially viable, income-generating projects became the more important focus and community development projects may also have suffered.

A major struggle for the Adivasis has been adjusting to a management style which conflicts with their own cultural patterns. Tribal people have always had a seasonal time orientation. Although AASSAV has attempted to develop within their own cultural organisational and management patterns, the demands of external forces and circumstances, such as donor and other partner expectations, have compelled AASSAV to compromise in order to operate within the expected parameters. Hence AASSAV works by the clock and the calendar, and fair remuneration for time worked demands time keeping, accounts and book keeping. Indigenous ways of managing development were never really taken seriously into consideration. These issues will be discussed further in the next chapter on Management.

With multiple donors, different reporting formats and different time frames for submission were often required, creating an administrative burden. A large portion of any NGO's management time and energy can be taken up in accounting systems, reducing the focus on the real work of development. A good financial manager could assist with the sophistication and complexity of the financial arrangements that have to be made by NGOs. For AASSAV, having lost their trained accounting staff three times and with only tribal membership, recruitment of people with skills is difficult. In a tribal community replacements are hard to find; there are no trained people available - a critical condition for the achievement of self-reliance. Eventually an administrator was found - Chapter 4 looks at this in more detail.

While the failure to achieve financial sustainability has been a disappointment, AASSAV gained much experience and knowledge through the practical development activities, which have been used as models for community development. Had there been no model plantations and farms, AASSAV would not have been in a position to operate in the community based programmes with the government, Naandi and CARE. While the new partnerships offered the hope of successful development in the region, many outsiders were involved in the management of them, which does not bode well for tribal independence. This has always been one of AASSAV's main aims and if it is going to be achieved, patience and perseverance on the part of the NGO partners will be required.

TOPICS FOR DISCUSSION

1. *'Perhaps development workers need to settle down to working slowly over time.'* Do you agree? Why/why not?

2. Is it fair to expect an NGO to be self-sustaining?

3. Is it justifiable to restrict the membership of an NGO to one indigenous group?

4. Discuss the impact of government bureaucracy on development initiatives.

5. Elucidate the statement: *'social change is...a prerequisite for bringing about sustainable development impact'.*

6. What would be an appropriate *'conscientisation processes'* in a tribal community?

7. In this chapter three different sorts of enterprises are referenced - projects decided upon and managed by an NGO, cooperative ventures, and individual entrepreneurship. Compare the benefits and drawbacks of each.

8. Relationships between the Naandi Foundation and AASSAV illustrate the uneven 'balance of power' between a tribal NGO and a business organisation. Are the pressures and pains (to the tribal group) an inevitable taste of the 'real world' to which they have to learn to 'shape up' or is there a fundamental injustice in the situation which needs to be moderated by government intervention?

9. AASSAV is participating in and helping to propel the momentum of a transitional social and economic system. In such circumstances how inevitable are hardships and set-backs? Who or what might be drawn in to facilitate a smoother adjustment of social and economic relationships?

CHAPTER 4

Structuring Local Ownership

"The essence of human dignity is self-reliance, the ability to manage one's own affairs. The essence of extreme poverty is dependence, being subject at every turn to forces utterly beyond one's control. Eradicating mass poverty should be the central purpose of development: partnership that promotes self-reliance should be the indispensable means."

For Whose Benefit? House of Commons, Government of Canada 1987

From the beginning, a central objective in establishing AASSAV was to see the Adivasi people become self-reliant, capable of managing their own development. The goal was to empower the people of AASSAV so that they in turn could empower others within their own community. AASSAV was thus established as a society owned and run by tribals. The insistence that membership and authority within the organisation be confined to locals did not exclude the possibility of others coming in to help in the development programme. Help was indeed essential, but help was to be directed at the growth in confidence and capacity of the tribal leaders themselves to manage their own affairs. In comparing AASSAV to other organisations Gustafsson argued that most NGOs

> *"tend to generate community empowerment through the educated people who run them. It is these who go out into the community and carry out development work; development is not produced by the people themselves. The link between [community development] and [the NGO] is a well-educated, highly skilled [group of people]."* (interview March 2002)

To work in the less conventional way suggested by Gustafsson *"took a long time and there were many leakages."* (ibid)

Cairns suggested that *"the experience and self-confidence acquired [through the self-management process]... should be seen as one of the most important results of the program to date"* (Evaluation Report 1993:4). He argued that this represented an *"important stage in strengthening the role and position of the Adivasi-Oriya tribal people"* in general.

How, then, did AASSAV structure its management patterns and how
effective was it in accomplishing the development goals of the
organisation? Did these structures build on, or conflict with, local
cultural norms? Why did the organisation have to restructure? Was it
due to pressure from outside or was it seen as necessary from within?

The Organisation

AASSAV set up three central management bodies to oversee the
functioning and effectiveness of the organisation: an executive
committee, an office of president, and a management team. For a long
time, AASSAV rejected the idea of having a governing body. It was
felt that this would not be conducive to developing local abilities as it
would be difficult for a Board to refrain from being paternalistic.
However, more recently a board was deemed necessary in order to
contract outside management expertise, one of the main objects of
employing outsiders being to train local capacity. Board members
would have to be selected carefully to ensure that the people chosen
would become learners of tribal culture as well as being ready to
contribute out of their skills to tribal management development. Board
members should not be there for self-interest and there would be no
remuneration; contributing to the development of self reliance in tribal
communities would have to be their reward. On the advice of Naandi
and others, a Board was formed.

The Executive Committee

The Executive Committee was made up of twelve members of the
Society who serve a fixed term although the time limit has yet to be
decided. It had never been determined as it was felt that elections
would only complicate the circumstances which arose following the
funding gaps. Since then, the position of AASSAV has rarely been
stable enough to hold elections. AASSAV's EC members were thus
appointed to represent a cross section of age, experience, education
and castes.

Meetings were held at least once a week, chaired by the president.
Minutes were handled by the Secretary and signed by all members
present. Besides decisions about projects, discussion on organisational
matters, the EC deals with the legal decisions needed for banks,
collaborative projects, staff disciplinary matters and appointments of
non-Adivasi management staff. Members meetings were also held
regularly to convey any new developments, to inform of new

appointments and to discuss project matters.

The Office of President

When it had been decided that a Society should be formed, the seven senior men who had been the Literacy Management Committee travelled to Visakhapatnam to submit their registration. They were accompanied by a government official from Paderu ITDA. When they arrived they found that registration regulations required the existence of an Executive Committee and so they hurriedly put one together at the office in Visakhapatnam. In line with their cultural norms, they put a committee together in terms of seniority and the most senior man, who was the first language assistant, became the president. Although he was knowledgeable and a good writer, he did not have the skills to manage the society and subsequently the committee agreed that a change was required. With the coordinator's help, they discussed what kind of person was needed to run AASSAV. They knew that someone should be nominated from their own members, but, again because of the cultural norms, no one made any recommendations. Although they all knew who would be the best person, the hierarchy within the tribal group and age of this person made an open choice impossible. The most suitable person was from one of the serving castes within the tribal community and he happened also to be a younger member of the group. Both factors excluded him from being chosen by the group for the presidency. In the end they asked the coordinator to choose for them and the young man chosen by the coordinator has from the start been, and continues to be, very committed to the work. He has had to overcome many social barriers in order to operate in the position he does. This has not been an easy process, but despite all the problems, he understands the business, has many good ideas, and is able to encourage AASSAV members as well as mobilise the communities. The struggle to win through and the personal achievement have been impressive and benefited both the Society and the tribal community.

Management Team

A wider team consisting of the head of each department and four members from outlying tribal areas meets once a month. At the meeting each reports on what the department has been doing and provides a written report, which includes a monthly financial report. Income and expenditures are discussed in detail so that all committee members understand the financial issues. It is in these committee sessions that decisions are made.

Income generation was not well understood within the tribal
community and new skills, attitudes and values were needed in order
for them to manage the work themselves. There were no models for
this within the tribal environment, and so new ways of operating took
time to learn. However they had been used to discussing all aspects of
the literacy project so there was something of a pattern for them as
they adjusted to the demands of their new roles. The committee
eventually learned to come to conclusions and decisions together rather
than waiting to be told what to do by the designated leader.

The management team was restructured as the new partnerships with
Naandi and Care developed and the way in which different aspects of
the work of AASSAV related to each other through the EC totally
changed.   The President, at first responsible for all aspects of
AASSAV's development and direction, was no longer in charge of the
processes as each project group became more autonomous.

As the changes occurred, there were many struggles for individuals
within the management team and for the members as a whole. The rest
of this chapter looks at the experiences they went through as they made
attempts to manage their own affairs.

Developing self-management

In the early years of the Society no specific process or plan was
followed and developing the managerial and organisational capacity of
AASSAV was a learning process in itself. The leaders responded to
the needs as they arose.   The way AASSAV needed to be managed
and the way the tribal people functioned were often at odds, but as they
gained in experience they eventually began to work more effectively
both individually and as a team.

Mentoring of the leaders, particularly by the coordinator, played a big
part in AASSAV's growth. During the literacy programme, the
coordinator never went anywhere alone; he was always accompanied
by at least one member, and often by a group, on every trip he made
for project shopping in Visakhapatnam or to government offices,
where they would sit in on discussions. The first time they were in the
Project Officer's office at ITDA together, the tribal people refused to
go in. Tribal people have certain rules of behaviour which they are
familiar with, but they had none for government offices! They felt
intimidated and shy, and were apprehensive of the way they might be
treated – often as inferior. But as they became used to the workings of
government, they became less inhibited and AASSAV staff were soon

visiting these places alone, working directly with government officials on all levels: local mandal offices, the agency headquarters in Paderu, District Headquarters in Visakhaptnam, Hyderabad (Andhra Pradesh state capital) and even in Delhi. As AASSAV leaders developed and became more used to the ways of government, and known in these offices, government officials also began to have more regard for them and showed them greater consideration.

As AASSAV developed into a more complex organisation, new administrative systems were required. To achieve this, people were brought in from outside to impart such skills as computing, accountancy and reporting, and to promote greater efficiency in management and organisation. Implementation of measures designed to improve efficiency was a difficult, sometimes a fraught, process. As Fowler (2001) points out, organisational behaviour imposed from outside is rarely effective or sustainable. Capacity must be built within the social and cultural context. Outsiders, including other Indian organisations, often have only a surface understanding of the tribal context. It is crucial to come alongside and encourage change through the cultural context rather than impose structures that take little or no account of the intricacies of tribal relationships. Growth in capacity is the result of gaining experience in a reciprocal manner: adapting exogenous ideas to the local cultural context and adjusting local cultural patterns in the light of the outside world. Changes of this kind take time and relationship and leadership struggles are an inevitable part of the process of adaptation.

Relationships

In tribal communities, authority is inherited, strongly hierarchical and normally vested in old and respected families. This was the way of the community leaders in the past, and continues in Indian societies today. Decisions cannot be authorised without the approval and consent of the leaders. Individual initiative is therefore rare. Those with social, religious or political power will take it for granted that their duty is to maintain it against external threats.

Some of those with inherited authority have natural leadership skills, others do not, and so in following local cultural patterns, AASSAV's appointments of people to leadership and management positions were sometimes successful, and sometimes not. Those who were not from traditional authority positions within the community had to overcome the barriers of birth and background to develop their leadership.

The president, as already indicated, was from one of the least respected groups and when he began with the literacy team, he was a shy young man, who would hardly speak at all. He was always a conscientious worker, committed to seeing this Society succeed, always on call and available any day of the week and any time. His skills and abilities developed over the years and his confidence and self-image grew correspondingly. He began to be driven around in a jeep and to wear a towel - a sign of authority. A telling mark of his new status came on the day a staff member came into the office and called him "Sir". It has always been difficult for him to be assertive in certain situations, however, particularly when faced with demanding government officials. Culture mandated that he acquiesce to their demands, which was not always in his or in the Society's interests.

Another committee member was clever and quick to grasp new things. He worked hard and was not afraid to learn or take responsibility, but with his group affiliation came a stigma that worked against his personal attributes and abilities. Among the younger educated staff caste differences *are* slowly being set aside, but they still have to contend with strong traditional views, attitudes and behaviours.

A particularly sensitive issue arises from the reality that much communication in business or government takes place in English. While Telugu is used almost universally in local government offices, English is the main means of communication outside the tribal area and with some of those who come in to help. Those who know English are frequently the youngest in the organisation causing difficulties with traditional tribal norms when senior members are dependent on translation by junior members.

AASSAV's policy is to give equal opportunity to everybody, whether women or men, from low caste or high caste. But there have been difficulties in maintaining this policy. Firstly, it has not been easy for AASSAV to employ women. One of the main reasons for this is that the relatively few educated tribal women are in high demand, particularly by the government. AASSAV states in its 2000 Final Report that it

> *"is ready to hire more female staff if and when applications are submitted and the applicant is eligible. The government and other NGOs are also looking for qualified women, and it is therefore not easy to hire more female staff."*

Two women had worked in the finance office of AASSAV, one woman was employed at the bank and three others were involved in the handicrafts training. Women are employed as labourers on the plantations and at the dairy farm, but these are few in number compared with the men. To have a woman employed in the bank was a decision that seemed particularly apposite since the bank is for women. But she was frequently absent, illustrating a more general problem: that women may be given a chance to work, but often they cannot sustain their commitment. The others who had been employed in computing, accounting and typing never stayed long enough to be given the opportunity to move into management. The realities make it difficult for women to take paid employment; when they marry they often have to move away, they have to look after the house and family and not only do they have to obey their husbands, they also have to obey their mothers-in-law.

Secondly, clan feeling is very strong, and even though these issues have been frequently discussed in the Executive Committee and efforts made to address them, difficulties remain. Many of the employees are related to each other, which at times leads to non-performance and indiscipline. It is difficult to take action against someone who is a relation or close friend, but omitting to do so creates a negative impact on both accountability and responsibility. The president himself is reluctant to discipline and, because of his background and his position, he has pressure put on him to grant certain benefits which are not his to give. The result of centuries of fixed hierarchies is that the right to give orders or even make requests will be resented or questioned if the person is younger or from an 'inferior' caste, clan or family. Tension arose from time to time between the president's office and the finance office, because the finance office was staffed by younger people. The president would spend money without going through the proper accounting channels and the finance office staff, because of their inferior status, could not tell the president that he should inform them of his spending. If the president wanted something, obedience to his will was essential for good relations to be maintained. It was, therefore, difficult to keep track of the finances and there were often clashes between the president and those hired from outside to keep accounting systems clear.

The principle is to see all men and women as equal and to give all of them a chance to prove themselves worthy of working with AASSAV and to reward all according to their input into the Society, not according to gender, family background or caste. And so it is vital that those in leadership are trained not to use their power to benefit one above another either within the Society or within the communities they are reaching. Although flexibility in attitudes in the face of the new demands of development is necessary, change is slow, sporadic and largely unpredictable.

Female employees

The following stories of two tribal women exemplify the significantly life-changing influence on women of, in the one case, the literacy classes and in the other, the job opportunity provided by AASSAV.

Chinnami had been faced with problems right from her young days. Her father died when she was born and her mother couldn't afford to send her to school. However, she had an uncle who encouraged her, and although he also had no money, they sold one pumpkin at summer rates and with that they purchased a slate. She was keen to learn, so the people of the village encouraged her to attend the literacy classes. She was the only female, but as she knew all the other learners and she was young, learning in an otherwise all male class was not a problem for her. She studied the same course for 3 years and when she was about 12 years old, she attended primary classes in a government school, as she was still young enough to register. She studied to 5th standard and then in 1994 she joined AASSAV. With the money she earned she went on to study until 10th standard on her own.

In 2001, she had been married for one year, but her husband had no work. They had had to move from their native place because of some disputes, but moving away from the family home brought isolation and lack of support. If she had not worked at the Society, it would have been hard for since they had no other source of income. This couple has since left the area: Chinnami has gone on to a government job and happily her husband is also working.

Laxmi attended school and studied up to 10th standard. Before joining the society she had to work very hard physically, on the land. As she sees it, it is better to work at the Society. Not only is it easier work but also more interesting: it has given her connections and activities outside the home and has expanded her horizons. Moreover working as a teacher at AASSAV gives her a status which she would not otherwise have, particularly as she is not married.

Decentralisation of power

In a community where hierarchy is important, the decentralisation of power is a major challenge. AASSAV attempted to develop a structure in which the leaders of the various departments could make decisions and take responsibility without having continually to refer to the president. But tribal cultural patterns made it difficult for the president to release the necessary authority and devolve responsibility: although he *said* he would be happy to do so, *actually* releasing control turned out to involve a mental paradigm shift that was fundamentally uncomfortable for him. Furthermore precisely because of the tribal peoples' shared 'template' for power structures, it is in practice more effective to give orders from the top.

Nonetheless, difficult and 'counter-cultural' though it might be, growth and expansion absolutely required decentralisation, so a new structure was formed and departments were set up to accommodate the various new development projects. The Coffee Project and CARE STEP each had its own manager, both appointed from outside the tribal communities, with AASSAV members working as part of each team. The cooperative bank had a head of banking, who was also an outsider. An outside manager was appointed to run the business programme and an outsider runs the finance office. The intention was that all who were appointed from outside were to train AASSAV members to run the offices and projects themselves. This has been a difficult process for both sides but, hopefully, over time, the sharing of power and decision-making will become more deeply rooted.

Restructuring and Reorganising

There had been no organised training in management skills for AASSAV personnel until, at the recommendation of CIDA, a management consultant was hired in 2001 to help with on-site management of the income-generating side of AASSAV. The new management consultant put new organisational and management structures in place, to facilitate the smoother functioning of all departments. All the changes were approved by the Executive Committee, personnel were reassigned and training took place. Thus, AASSAV embarked on changes towards more efficient and effective working practices.

The new procedures were explained in meetings where the EC and members were present, taking care to underline that the changes would be implemented gradually. The changes were all accepted, but still the reality when they came to be implemented was a shock for the members of AASSAV, the EC and especially the president, who, until now, had had almost total control of all the departments. Although there were positive results from the appointment of a manager who would instigate the changes, the process of introducing the changes and building ownership for them proved less than straightforward.

The division of work was a necessary change. The president had always dealt with financial matters, including loans and salaries, as well as personnel and projects, but as the organisation grew, it was no longer an efficient way to operate. Now each department would send its financial reports to the finance office rather than to the president's office. These changes were intended to help AASSAV avoid some of the difficulties of the past. For example, the president was often away and responses to government, national or international organisations needed to be immediate. Now the administrator would have the authority to deal with most queries, which would allow the day to day operating of the Society to continue in the president's absence. The president would be freed up to concentrate on his official duties, such as government relations, NGO relations, training, and plantation supervision, which was also where he functioned at his best: relating to, motivating and leading communities in development.

A second change was in streamlining AASSAV membership. It had at one time over 200 staff members who had been faithfully paid, even when there was no work. Up to this point, AASSAV had operated as a development NGO, dependent on funding, and not as a business. Its attitude towards its members was one of care, respecting and honouring their tribal roots, as well as their background of poverty and marginalisation. But the question arose over whether the "over-caring" attitudes that had existed in the past could be tolerated if AASSAV was to become self-reliant and self-sustaining. Rather it would be necessary to scale down and lay off staff. Although this was done honourably, by dismissing those who were irregular in attendance, or who were of retirement age, it was still a culture shock. AASSAV had always allowed families to replace a family member who retired, or died, although the Society was not legally obligated to do this unless AASSAV land originally belonged to that family. This practice ceased to operate and people became contract workers rather than fully paid members. Thus by these various means membership was reduced by at least fifty. At the same time, what had always been the theory - that if no work was available to staff in their own particular sector, other work would be assigned to them - was to be enforced as the practical modus operandi.

Attempting to institute modern business methods and business-like performance was a challenge for both consultant and staff. As a tribal organisation AASSAV had always taken tribal needs and concerns into consideration, but local ways of functioning are not necessarily compatible with modern business practices. Traditional tribal values do not give preference to efficiency, time management and cost effectiveness as business does. Decisions were not always made necessarily in the best interests of the Society, but rather in the interests of individuals or communities, or in to maintain good relationships. Time keeping, taking personal responsibility for the work, meeting deadlines for getting information and reports out, were all part of the new management operations. Now there was a firmer trend towards making decisions that opposed cultural patterns where necessary - some of the old was sacrificed to incorporate the new. AASSAV leaders had to make decisions on how best to achieve the goals and purposes of AASSAV, while at the same time preserving their tribal roots and links.

While there are thoroughly legitimate reasons for tempering the full implementation of hard-headed business practices, they do not always work well in remote tribal areas where employment opportunities are limited and tribal people have to live and work together within their own communities. An approach that does not connect sympathetically with tribal realities can backfire, reducing the sense of community ownership of AASSAV and its work. If the social and cultural norms are upset, giving rise to a sense of grievance, AASSAV may not be able to function well. Cultures change slowly, as they come face to face with new ways, and so it is with AASSAV and the communities it serves.

It was anticipated that having an 'outsider' as administrator, who was from another part of India and not a member of a tribal group, would have certain clear advantages. Relationships within village communities mean that one person cannot normally tell another what to do if that would run counter to their customary hierarchical relational structure. An outsider who is not part of these relational networks and give instructions to anyone. The procedure was that when advice was given by the administrator, the EC would discuss and modify where necessary. They would then endorse the changes and support the new manager in implementing them.

However, although the changes had been discussed and endorsed, the manner in which they were then implemented often seemed like an imposition and the changes were not well received. There were suspicions, based on deep-rooted resentments on the part of the tribal people against incomers. This was understandable as, after plains people first arrived, tribal land and livelihoods were quickly destroyed, and tribal people, having little access to education, were oppressed and exploited. On the other hand there were negative attitudes toward tribal people, who are commonly stereotyped as ignorant, uncivilised, dirty, drunkards, work-shy and incapable of forward planning. The administrator's perception was that several people did not like what he was doing and were actively working against him. Not surprisingly then, misunderstandings and antagonisms surfaced from time to time between the new administrator and AASSAV staff and members.

It had been agreed from the beginning that whoever was employed as administrator should learn the tribal language and be able to communicate in that as soon as possible. But he was not even a Telugu speaker and therefore was not able to communicate with the AASSAV staff in anything other than in English. Translation was required, which was awkward for the young interpreter, because the giving of orders to senior members, even through translation, was considered improper. It was a set of circumstances inherently likely to give rise to misunderstandings and tensions. If there had been a common language, the president and EC could have been fully involved in the changeover to the new system. As it was, the president in particular felt excluded as change, much of which he did not understand, went on around him. The result was a division between the administrative office and the president's office, an issue which was not adequately dealt. Tensions also arose among the members which grew into a revolt, involving mainly members from outlying plantations.

In November 2001 a group of angry AASSAV members arrived at the HQ shouting "Go home!" threatening to kill the new administrator. Although the problems with the finances were not his fault and the new agreements had been put before the members by the Executive Committee and agreed to by the members, it now became apparent that too many modifications in pay had been instituted at the same time. The main complications were due to the previous funding gap of 18 months. During this time AASSAV had explained the situation to the merchants who had given loans, and members had undertaken to repay their debts when the funds arrived. As AASSAV members had not paid all their debts, appropriate amounts were taken off their salaries to repay the merchants directly. On top of this, every year until now, members had been given a 10% pay increase and a "bonus". This year, because of the shortage of funds, neither the increase nor the bonus was included.

Most of the labouring members of AASSAV were almost entirely dependent on their job, having no land themselves. It was therefore understandable that they should rebel, but it was unlikely that they would have done so, it was suggested, without incitement; elements both within and outside the membership may have created the disturbance.

The focus for the protesters' anger was the new administrator because he had been the one attempting to sort out AASSAV's finances. In response to the revolt, the 10% increase was restored, AASSAV leaders thereby agreeing that there was too much pressure on members in managing their personal finances.

After this episode the administrator no longer attempted to make changes in the management of AASSAV. He felt that the EC had not given him sufficient support, so he simply continued to maintain AASSAV's accounts.

At the meeting following the rebellion, the coordinator, attempting to defuse the situation, strongly advised them not to attack anyone again, and that the correct procedure was to take their grievances to the committee. A letter written at the time stated that "*if they had not employed the new administrator, there would have been no funds at all from Canada to take them this far.*" The administrator had worked hard to set these measures in place and it was not his fault that changes had to be made; it was the responsibility of the EC.

Where international money is involved, there is often a sense of mistrust and not properly understand the situation, the plantation workers thought that those at the centre were taking it for themselves. They did not understand that in order to survive changes had to be made.

> "*They only think about whether they are getting their money; they are only interested in whether they are getting as much as possible. They are not educated and do not have an understanding of the ways things work at the headquarters.*"

> (Vice President speaking after the event.)

The perspective of the administrator was that he had been unable to work effectively in the situation not only because of misunderstandings based on miscommunications but that there was a resistance to change among the leadership. He said that when the coordinator was away it was hard to get anyone to do anything. The people would not respond to him without the coordinator's backing and he felt unsupported by the president. AASSAV had a new structure, but no help to see it through. In 2004 after training local people to carry on, the administrator visited once a year to assist in auditing the accounts.

A constant problem is that of Headquarters staffing. For example, two young men had been trained to do the monitoring, evaluation and reporting. They had overcome the potential barriers of being young, convent-educated and English speakers, and were beginning be well established in this work. But because of their English language ability, they had to be moved to help the new administrator. One was assigned to Personnel, the other to Materials and Supplies. It was difficult for AASSAV to find suitable replacements for the monitoring and evaluation work.

Developing the next generation of leaders has been fraught with difficulties. This has been so, not only because of the traditional leadership patterns, nor that trainees would not have made good leaders but because AASSAV jobs have not been seen as secure or high status - not as secure as government jobs and not as high status as employment in the cities. Naturally, many took advantage of their training to seek more prestigious jobs for which, by virtue of their training, they were now qualified.

Organisational Strengths and Weaknesses

As with any organisation AASSAV has certain strengths which need to be built on. There are also many weaknesses, some of which are due to cultural practices and some to the difficult circumstances AASSAV operates under.

Strengths

One of AASSAV's main strengths has been that staff and the communities share the same culture and language enabling positive communication and understanding. The organisational has been accepted by Adivasi and non-Adivasi alike and a good name has been established among government officials, NGOs and the general public both in its commitment to development and in financial accounting. AASSAV leaders have learned to negotiate with government, business and other NGO leaders. Government has shown sufficient interest in AASSAV to support it with business and involve it in development work. National NGOs have contracted to work with AASSAV (CARE India, Naandi) and International Development Agencies speak highly of AASSAV. AASSAV has been given recognition by high government officials as an agency that will see development projects through to success.

With all its experience AASSAV has become an agency with

considerable knowledge relating to development issues in the area, an understanding of public relations with government, NGOs and business and experience in interacting with village communities. With eighteen years in the management of projects and programmes AASSAV has learned from its successes as well as from its mistakes and failures.

The new partnership with Naandi and the move towards participatory development with CARE STEP is using all of AASSAV's previous experience in development, training, management and local relationships. It is certain that, without its considerable experience built up over the years, AASSAV would not have been able to take on these new partnerships.

Weaknesses

Many of the weaknesses within AASSAV arose from the attempt to bring together two different ways of operating. Adivasi culture is orientated around the seasons is a positive factor within the culture, but a negative factor in project based organisations. Staff took unplanned leave, according to the social pattern of tribal life, creating an obvious difficulty in implementing AASSAV's management and operating systems. There is little concept of long-range planning when for generations life has been lived day to day. Related to this is a lack of understanding of financial planning. Until recently, trading with money was unknown; only goods and services were offered. In tribal life relationship takes precedence over project or task and so implementing projects at the expense of relationships is not easily accepted and Adivasi culture is not assertive in nature, which is positive in small rural communities closely dependent on each other for survival, but it is a hindrance in negotiating with government and outside agencies. Modern technological practices are not part of Adivasi life and modern business practices are not understood.

Another problem is the tendency for office staff to copy the practices of government officials. In government offices, responsibilities are strictly delineated. Everything is kept under lock and key to prevent tampering with files. It is a typical frustration to many to find that only one official will deal with a particular matter and if he happens to be absent no one else can help. The AASSAV staff often behave in the same way and, with no other model, such behaviour is difficult to counteract.

Other weaknesses derive from the general lack of access to education and training among the tribal communities. AASSAV has been unable to retain a committed core of well-educated and trained staff and it is difficult to replace them with other tribal people. Since 1988, when AASSAV was established, over 100 staff left or were dismissed. Many of these had been trained by AASSAV in areas such as typing (12), electrical work (1), sales (3), training in hotel management (5), in carpentry (2), printing (2), computers (4), accounts (5), and in tailoring (1). Others who already had training were hired for senior positions and many of these also left. These people could do their jobs well; they could take initiative and make decisions. Twenty out of the twenty-three who left for government jobs were trained by AASSAV. A government job is a job for life and it comes with a pension and AASSAV cannot compete with this in terms of status and job security.

A large number left during the times AASSAV experienced extended periods of financial need. Twenty-six left during one extended funding gap, compounding AASSAV's problems. The print shop manager, for example, was a person who could take initiative and make decisions. He was on the executive committee and he was good at public speaking. He would show visitors around and was well able to speak on behalf of AASSAV. He left to become a teacher: had he stayed, it is likely that the finance office could have been run competently in his hands. Since then new accountants have had to be trained, not once, but twice.　There are few tribals in the area who have enough education to be trained and so the fact that AASSAV has not yet achieved self-management is hardly surprising. The journey towards self-management would have been much more rapid if AASSAV had been able to retain trained staff. It is sad that there is no support for retaining staff in an organisation whose unique value lies in the fact that is closely related to the people and their development and it is even more unfortunate that Government officials even encourage employees to leave and work in government offices for the reserved positions.

Impact of external circumstances

There were other difficulties which AASSAV has had to face:

1. Banking operations were extremely slow and often delayed:

   ▪ A round trip of 100kms was required to make any transactions and cheque clearances often took weeks.

   ▪ Repeated requests had to be made for bank statements which also took a long time to receive.

- Money transfers to and from the city had to be done by draft for security and speed. This involved a staff member's time and additional expense.

- Telephone and fax communications from the Headquarters have been installed only in March 2002, but international dialling facilities were unavailable and internet facilities erratic.

- Poor electricity: cuts, failures and low voltage. The service improved somewhat over the years and AASSAV had to install a generator for daytime use when necessary; expensive in running costs.

- The poor quality of manufactured goods purchased (pumps, jeep parts, etc) meant that parts often had to be replaced.

- Jeep parts not always available locally; they had to be brought from Visakhapatnam which could take two or more days.

- Every time a computer or other machine went wrong engineers had to be brought from Visakhapatnam.

- There are often extreme delays in government offices for normal transactions, which could be done immediately.

- Extreme delays in payment of bills by government departments.

While many of these realities are beyond AASSAV's control and simply had to be lived with, they were a significant constraint on the organisation's development, consuming valuable time, personnel, resources and increasing the already high administrative and running costs.

The role of an expatriate

The literacy programme and the subsequent transformation of that initiative into a local NGO started through the intervention of Uwe and Elke Gustafsson, who with his family had lived in the tribal village of Hattaguda since 1970. They did not leave except for short breaks until 30 years later when illness compelled them to return to Canada. It is clear that their role was central, which gives rise to a number of questions about the presence of an expatriate over such a length of time. How far did he retain control? What about cultural influences, witting or unwitting? How could the power differential between a Canadian-educated German and a marginalized Indian tribal group be bridged without nefarious effects of domination, unbalanced expectations, suspicion or mistrust?

The nature of the work Gustafsson came to do meant that listening, learning and cooperation were essential right from the start. Linguistic research and language development could only be done with the help, support and involvement of the local community. Gustafsson encouraged the introduction of literacy and adult education programmes, and supported the establishment and development of the tribal organisation, but the project was always the community's project. This is easily said, but what is the evidence that it was so? What were the problems and conflicts along the way?

Gustafsson uses the word 'privilege' to describe the opportunity he and his wife have had to work with the local community. They took the view that, as outsiders, they needed to learn. The tribal people are the masters in their own environment.

> *"They take me to the jungle and I am lost. I don't know one tree from another. I don't know the names or the potential of these trees. They know all of this. I come as a learner. When we learn something from them we are very grateful for what we have learned. I am always delighted when I learn even a new word." (Gustafsson, Interview 2002)*

Organisations set up to benefit the disadvantaged rarely involve the beneficiaries themselves in the work, but the Gustafssons consciously sought at all times to engage the tribal people in decision-making. The committee members were encouraged to take responsibility for decisions and so, during the literacy years, the Literacy Management Team learned how to manage and organise the work themselves.

When AASSAV was established, however, a new way of operating was required for which no one was prepared. The demands were new to the Gustafssons as well as to the team; they had to learn together. However, being more familiar with the procedures of organisations, Gustafsson in effect managed the project for the first two years while seeking to model and mentor local staff. The many years of association with the people, fluency in the local language and a desire to continue learning local cultural patterns, were factors that supported this process. From January 1990, two years after the Society was formed, Gustafsson no longer chaired any meetings. The AASSAV leadership to take on the management responsibilities and the executive committee and members' meetings since that time have been led by the president. Gustafsson took on the role of Coordinator.

AASSAV staff did most of the planning and supervision alone. When Gustafsson was present, his main focus was one of explanation, encouragement and exhortation, explaining new developments within AASSAV such as the management changes and reorganisation, and the partnerships with national and international NGOs (CARE, CIDA and Naandi). Descriptive report writing is still a major hurdle for the EC and team and Gustafsson took the main responsibility for this, although all information is prepared by the relevant departments.

Because the prevailing attitudes towards tribal communities in mainstream society tend towards superiority, Gustafsson's role in guarding the aims and values of the Society remained an important one as the project expanded and new partners were introduced. New partners, rather than supporting indigenous ways and developing the skills and abilities of the tribal people to take on the management roles, tended to take control, leaving the tribal people to follow their lead.

There is a fine line between offering too much advice and giving too little. The one inhibits the development of indigenous decision making, and the other leaves the tribal leadership facing unfamiliar experiences with inadequate understanding. Acquiring the skills and abilities to make decisions, many of them sophisticated and not part of tribal society and culture, has demanded an experiential learning process requiring time and patience, for tribal team and for Gustafsson.

There is general agreement that the work of the Gustafssons in this tribal region has had a great impact. The tribal group would not have advanced as far as they have if the language and literacy programme had not been initiated. An organisation like AASSAV run and managed by tribal people would not have existed without the strengthened cultural self-esteem and confidence which the language and literacy programme fostered. It is acknowledged by government just how highly the Gustafssons are respected by the people for their work for them and on their behalf.

Cairns noted in his report in 1997 that

> "*AASSAV's present status is attributable to the guidance and support of Uwe Gustafsson, Project Co-ordinator. In the overall development of AASSAV, in discussions, meetings and in administrative, financial and structural issues, Mr Gustafsson has provided advice and support, but has by the present phase given almost complete responsibility to Tribal Society officials themselves. This has enabled them, in a relatively short period, to gain experience and confidence in the planning, administration and management of the overall programme and in negotiations with Indian government officials.*" (5)

The persistent determination of one person often drives a vision or an organisation and although Gustafsson is not an official leader of this organisation, he has been the inspiration behind it since the beginning. Living in the community, developing a knowledge of the language and culture, working closely with the local people, in particular those who became the four Chief Project Supervisors, have all been factors crucial in bridging the gap between expatriate workers, national and international development agencies, the government of India and local communities. Elke Gustafsson's work with the sick and the poor (described in more detail below) further enhanced their rapport with the people.

While the tribal leaders themselves maintain that it was Gustafsson who instilled in them the purpose and resolve to achieve, it was also clear that the cooperation of the four tribal men who helped from the beginning played a very significant role in the success of the literacy project and, later, in the establishment of AASSAV. Their advice was critical in many significant decisions, particularly those concerning traditional cultural values, norms and behaviours which strengthened the project at a local level.

Although gradually withdrawing, the coordinator's presence and involvement remained necessary, particularly in the coordination of new projects and in developing links with the funding agencies. As relationships grew between AASSAV and the outside world through NGO partnerships, Gustafsson had to ensure that the capacity of the tribal leadership to continue to lead was not undermined but rather developed positively under the new circumstances and conditions. AASSAV was essential to the outside NGOs if their work in the tribal communities was to continue, but these partnerships have not always been easy and tension develops at times and Gustafsson has often had to negotiate between the partners. As he withdraws, it is to be hoped that all groups will have developed the understanding, attitudes and skills which will allow growth of AASSAV and its leaders to continue.

The coordinator and his family have made a huge investment in this work and looking back over his many years of engagement with this community, Gustafsson states that it is the long haul that is necessary. There is both a cost and a benefit: living in the villages is not always straightforward or easy, but it gives opportunity to mix with the people and to work towards the goal with a determined commitment. This approach is in some ways old-fashioned and could so easily have become a neo-colonial relationship. It was perhaps the recognition, from the start, that local culture and knowledge are of intrinsic value that sent the message that local leadership and management were both possible and right.

Chambers (1983) states that

> "...*self-confidence cannot be taught, it must be acquired. Self-confidence is acquired through positive experience, through small successes reinforcing each other. Self-confidence can be promoted through expressions of confidence and encouragement. It is destroyed by attitudes of superiority and negative criticism. Development workers must avoid attitudes and comments, which reinforce feelings of inferiority. They must show that they appreciate the poor as individuals and respect their knowledge and judgement. Development workers who do not have a fundamental belief in the abilities of the poor will not be successful.*" (53)

The dominant partner in any relationship has to take great care not to use that power to control, but to the benefit of the growth and development of the people.

The impact of a foreign woman

One aspect of the work that had a great impact on the communities and gave the Gustafsson family a good rapport with the people was that from the beginning they cared for the sick and needy. At first this was very much a shared responsibility between Uwe and Elke, but when AASSAV was established, Elke handled almost all this side of the work on her own. She has been instrumental in the treatment, care and recovery of many people in the tribal area. She accompanied patients to the hospitals in Araku Valley, Visakhapatnam and Asha Kiran (a mission hospital 60kms from Hattaguda in the State of Orissa). Following treatment by doctors, Elke would do the aftercare from their home. There was hardly a time when their backyard did not have patients during the daytime. Many of the cases were serious (especially TB) and these patients would not be alive today if it had not been for Elke.

Laksmi lived across from the Gustafssons' home. She contracted TB when she was still quite young. It was spinal TB and already she was almost bent over double. Elke, Gustafsson's wife, literally carried her out of the jeep into the government TB hospital in Visakhapatnam. Usually members of the family will stay at the hospital to look after the patient, but in this case no one would go. So Elke herself stayed there to make sure that the doctor's orders were carried out, and the injections and medicines were given at the proper time. When this course was finished, she brought Laksmi back to Hattaguda where she stayed with her brother. Her husband had sent her out because she could no longer work. She was carefully nursed back to health, with good meals and the required medication. In fact, if it had not been for Elke's persistence and care in nursing and feeding her, Laksmi would not be alive today.

To keep her busy, Elke taught her to read and write to the point of passing the AASSAV exam. When Laksmi was strong enough to walk again, Elke personally talked to the Project Officer at ITDA to add Laksmi to the list of trainees for sewing course. She was not one of the ten selected for the ITDA funded programme, but it was felt very strongly that she should learn a skill. Elke moved the wheels of government and eventually she was admitted to the class. She joined AASSAV in 1992 as a member of the sewing centre staff. She was given a sewing machine by the government and so was able to take on outside work, stitching blouses and other ladies' clothes.

Another example is **Zogubandu**, a staff member in the print shop.

The Gustafssons were called to his home in Hattaguda one day, having been told that he was very sick. When they saw him, he was a skeleton of a man, obviously suffering very much. Zogubandu had a wife and four young daughters who expected him to die at any moment.

The Gustafssons asked his family if they could transport him to Asha Kiran, a Christian Hospital in Koraput, Orissa, sixty kilometres away. They agreed and Elke took the jeep and a driver and off they went. Elke left him in the hospital where they first of all put him on IV and then pumped two litres of pus out of his abdomen. He had intestinal obstruction and although they operated, they did not have much hope of his survival. But he hung on to life and very slowly gained some strength. Eventually, the doctors felt they could send him home as Elke would do the postoperative care and to everyone's amazement, Zogubandu arrived back in the village.

The important job of keeping the wound clean with sterile dressings then began. Elke did the sterilization in her kitchen. Morning and evening she went to their home. She also took care of the feeding process, preparing the famous nine-grain cereal, and feeding him herself. Zogubandu steadily improved and gained strength.

When the Gustafssons were to leave for Canada, Elke taught his nephew how to do the dressings. The wound had closed but still needed to be dressed and so she prepared enough sterile dressing materials to last.

Before leaving Elke took a promise from him and his wife, "Now that I am leaving, you must promise me that you will send all four daughters to school." They promised and they did send them to school.

Elke encouraged parents to send their children to school. Some were sent to local schools, others to boarding schools and the impact of education on the community over the years has been considerable.

Caring for the sick in a place where access to health care was limited, where poverty exacerbated the recovery process and both successes and failures occurred, Elke's health itself finally reacted. The case which caused her so much apprehension concerned a baby. Philip and his wife Nirmala, both MDs, happened to be visiting the Gustafssons when a mother brought her sick baby in. Philip and Nirmala had no hope at all of her survival, but Elke took little Pormilla and her mother to the hospital, where they stayed nine days until the baby was over the worst. When they came home, the mother was uncooperative and would not learn to look after the baby, so morning and afternoon the baby was brought to Elke for feeding. Despite the mother's defiance, carelessness and neglect, the baby survived, but it was following this episode that the Gustafssons decided that they would have to return home. In 2000, after 30 years in the village, they left. Uwe Gustafsson returns for two months twice a year and it may be in due course that Elke will again visit.

Conclusions

AASSAV has made some astonishing changes in the last few years as it has grown from a small unknown organisation working in literacy, to an organisation in demand by government and outside donor agencies. The achievements have been outstanding, bearing in mind above all that AASSAV is an entirely tribal organisation, consisting of members who were for so long marginalized and ignored by mainstream society. For example:

- In 1988 none of the leadership and staff could have visited government offices or dealt with business establishments in the city except with some other non-Adivasi personnel. Now these visits are made almost entirely by the AASSAV staff.

- AASSAV has been accepted as an NGO in its own right and is invited to attend government functions, seminars and discussions on development issues.

- Government and business representatives treat AASSAV leadership and staff with respect.

- Government and business relations are almost completely accomplished by AASSAV leadership and staff.

- Government and business representatives no longer want to see the coordinator first, but in most cases approach AASSAV leadership directly.

- Correspondence from government and business is now mostly addressed to the AASSAV president or secretary at the AASSAV address, rather than to the Coordinator.

The process of change has often been radical for the tribal people and few, inside or outside the group, have fully understood the implications. Bringing outsiders into the organisation was a deliberate strategy to challenge old behaviours and bring new perspectives as there was little knowledge or experience of how things could be done differently within the organisation itself to engender change. However, those who were brought in to facilitate change should have been able to deal with the complexities of the interface between the modern world and the traditions of the local community. It is rare to find the appropriate attitude and tribal people are sensitive to negative and superior attitudes. Trusting outsiders was a difficult proposition for communities who have faced years of marginalisation by the majority community. Developing a positive relationship with the people has been a priority and only in this way can an outsider gain the confidence of the tribals.

The need for change was usually understood, but still it was not easy to make that change when the old way of working was much closer to the relational dynamics of tribal society. There was resistance to change and there were power struggles, particularly where traditional roles were being challenged. To dismantle the hierarchical structure and develop new patterns of authority was a difficult process.

Even the coordinator, whose intention it was to withdraw gradually as the restructuring process became a part of AASSAV, found the changes challenging, as the new outsiders became part of the everyday life of AASSAV. In retrospect it would seem that too much internal change was demanded all at once. But, on the other hand, if AASSAV had not been willing to change, it was likely that it would cease to exist. Outside agencies would not have the long term patience of the coordinator. Top-down imposition of change however is unlikely to work if the literature – and experience - of development is to be believed. Will AASSAV survive in its current form? Will it continue to have any practical purpose and function and if not, what shape will it take?

The next chapter looks at the partnership processes which AASSAV has been through, asking questions concerning what makes a true partner and how true partnership can be achieved through markedly different cultures as required in the context of development.

TOPICS FOR DISCUSSION

1. Do you agree that *'the essence of human dignity is self-reliance'*?

2. Do you agree that most NGOs *'tend to generate community empowerment through the educated people who run them'*?

3. Discuss the implications of tribal concepts of caste and other hierarchies of status for 'modernising' organisations.

4. What is the relationship between education and self-confidence? Which is more influential as a motor of social and economic improvement?

5. How may efficient organisation and modern management techniques be best implemented in an organisation staffed by tribal people and dedicated to their betterment?

6. What are the pressures towards centralised control and 'top-down' management in a tribal society? How might countervailing influences be brought to bear?

7. Traditional tribal society functions with a high level of interdependency based on custom. When a new type of relationship emerges based on strictly contractual employment and wages, how far is it possible and how far is it desirable to perpetuate the complex 'net' of family and tribal social obligations? Or are the two economic systems in principle incompatible?

8. Is there a case for government intervention to make it more attractive for skilled indigenous workers to stay in their localities rather than seek advancement in the cities?

9. What should be the role of an expatriate in local development?

CHAPTER 5
Maintaining Local Control

This chapter looks at AASSAV's experiences, their struggles and achievements as they developed relationships with government, donors, and national and international NGOs. It analyses the positive and negative aspects of the partnerships and explains how AASSAV changed through these relationships.

Partners in Development

Genuine partnerships, based on mutual respect, where collaboration and participation are central and where each has the opportunity to develop a positive understanding of the other, particularly in cross cultural situations, are not easy to form. The dominant partner is often the funding agency, with tendencies to prescribe projects and exert control over implementation, requiring results within a particular time frame and rarely taking into account the intricacies of local organization and circumstances.

Genuine partnerships, in fact, take time and effort, a factor which is rarely built into any development schedule. As Chambers (1983) points out:

> *Where there is genuine participation, mistakes will be made; there will be failures and there will be progress – a few steps forward, a step or two back. Participation is essentially a "learning by doing" exercise – plans are made, action is taken, results are studied, lessons are learned and new plans and actions take place (57).*

In the case of AASSAV, however, a positive relationship had already been established between the literacy management group and the coordinator and it was he who made the link between them and the international donors possible. At first, the donors neither made strong demands, nor provided constructive input and it was the coordinator who guided AASSAV and who reported back to the donors. Thus it was the local team, with the coordinator acting as advisor, who essentially made plans and implemented them.

As a fully indigenous organisation, AASSAV was able to assist government and other outside agencies in gaining the confidence of local communities to participate in their own development. Without this, outside agencies would have found it difficult to bring about effective development. The experience required for effective development to take place, however, depended on building the capacity of AASSAV, which, in turn, could not have been done without the assistance of outside agencies. The following looks at how this experience was acquired.

District and local government agencies

The Government of Andhra Pradesh introduced a policy in March 1997 aimed at involving local communities more closely in the development process. This policy encouraged greater decision-making by the people and the involvement of grassroots organisations, and in this deliberate effort to establish participatory planning at the village level, it was hoped that the effectiveness of development programmes would be increased. Formerly, the relationship between NGOs and government was one of suspicion; they even appeared at times to be in competition, but now it was hoped that more positive relationships could be established. Government officials and other stakeholders in the development process needed to increase their understanding of the local situation and, with this end in view NGOs would act as a bridge between the local constituency and cultural context and outside agencies. It was hoped that even though they were working alongside government, NGOs would maintain their local identity and carry the confidence of the local communities.

AASSAV had developed strong links with the Adivasi people and had won credibility within the community through its language work and literacy programmes. With an entirely indigenous leadership, AASSAV had the ability to communicate effectively and relate positively in the local communities. Knowing the tribal language and culture meant that access to indigenous resources and knowledge and the understanding of local circumstances and conditions were all straightforward.

From the beginning, the Literacy Management Group worked closely with district and local government agencies, and after the establishment of AASSAV, the authorities were kept closely informed of everything that was being done. It was, in fact, a Project Officer at the ITDA who encouraged the Literacy Management team to establish a Society. It was openly stated that AASSAV could reach the Adivasi people more effectively than the government could and the Society was recognised as a competent implementer of development programmes among the Adivasi people. Thus it was that AASSAV became an active partner implementing many of the government's development activities for the tribal people. Although, due to a variety of reasons which was discussed in Chapter 3, the effectiveness of the projects varied, AASSAV members grew in confidence and ability through its government partnerships.

AASSAV's main government partners were the Integrated Tribal Development Agency (ITDA) and the District Rural Development Agency (DRDA).

Integrated Tribal Development Agency (ITDA)

ITDA is a government agency which was specifically set up to address the development needs of the tribal people within their agency areas. The ITDA offices are based at Paderu a distance of 50kms from AASSAV headquarters. The AASSAV president and vice president are often invited to meetings hosted by ITDA in Paderu for discussions about development and training programmes funded by various donor agencies. AASSAV and ITDA have collaborated together over many projects and they have had good relationships with the various project officers.

ITDA-AASSAV Collaborative Projects have included:

- Five one-year training courses for adolescent girls called Vanitha Velugu Bata (Girls' Training Course) from 1994-2000.

- Coffee Planting Project involving 1300 farmers on 1400 acres. AASSAV raised 1,200,000 coffee plants in coffee nurseries and managed the planting on the plantations between 1999-2000.

- AASSAV hosted the Project Officers of four districts for a workshop.

- Women's training course.

District Rural Development Agency (DRDA)

DRDA is one of the government's main channels for rural development. The MPDO (Mandal Parishad Development Office) is the office at local government level where DRDA's development programmes in the mandals are implemented. Village development officers (VDOs – now abolished) worked for the MPDO implementing the projects in the communities.

AASSAV maintained good relationships with the DRDA's Project

Directors, who in turn were supportive of AASSAV's work. The local mandal development officers have a high regard for AASSAV, speaking well of the hard work of the president and its members. AASSAV staff often accompanied VDOs into the communities when discussions about the implementation of programmes took place. Most VDOs did not speak the local language, and there was latent distrust by the communities of government officials. It was much easier for both the local community and for the government official when an AASSAV member was involved in a liaison role.

AASSAV conducted several training courses for DRDA through the MPDO including bee keeping, production of tamarind products and turmeric powder and vegetable cultivation. While the training was positive, ongoing support for those who had been trained - to develop a small business for example - was limited. Follow-up is essential if training is to be effective, and this is one of the areas where government programmes often fail to take root. One of the main reasons for this is that directors of the various government departments stay in their position for a limited time and the projects implemented by one director are rarely followed up by the next.

Women's self-help groups were also established by DRDA under a national scheme called Development of Women and Children in Rural Areas (DWCRA). These groups were primarily linked to cooperative societies that manage savings and loan programmes. DRDA provided training in income generation, health and literacy for the DWCRA groups. DWCRA and self help groups (SGH), gave women an organisation for themselves providing them with a positive status in their male dominated world. AASSAV hoped that, besides increasing their income, these groups will soon be in a position to promote literacy for the women and that women would no longer be ignored in development activities in their own villages. The women themselves are aware - and have openly stated - that together they have more power, enabling them, for example, to put pressure on those men who would drink any extra money. Amazingly, the men have been very supportive of the women's self-help groups as they see the contribution women can make to family and community well-being. More income is being generated, there is increasing access to services and families are becoming more positive about their futures.

AASSAV conducted training for 240 young girls, most of whom were school dropouts, with funding from ITDA (see above). They attended the AASSAV centre for one year where they learned skills as well as literacy. During that year a wide range of visitors came to see the training, including government officers, with whom the girls interacted. Having contact for a year with people outside their villages where they were praised and encouraged, made a big difference to their self-confidence. These young women could potentially have an impact in their own villages if guidance and support were maintained. AASSAV requested that some kind of support continue so that the girls could use their learning in income generating projects. One of the ways in which the communities could benefit from their training was through the DWCRA and self help groups and it was suggested that one trainee representing three villages should be sent to the DRDA training centre near Visakhapatnam. Inevitably many of the girls who trained would soon have been married and with children to look after would be restricted by their family duties; but DWCRA groups are ideal for village women in their current circumstances.

AASSAV was approached by DRDA in 2000 to run the cooperative bank for the DWCRA groups in the local area. AASSAV agreed to this, although they were aware that much support and training would be needed to build up the expertise of the tribal people involved in running it. In the event problems occurred in providing sufficient training to the bank staff, particularly in giving and reclaiming loans. Loans were given without sufficient knowledge of the group situation and financial losses were incurred. There was also pressure from government officials and from their own people to give loans without proper security. Naandi, who were supporting AASSAV in the coffee project and wanted to use the bank for the farmer's cooperatives, was then approached and agreed to support the bank on the condition that they had full managerial control, but to this there were objections by both government officials and AASSAV leaders, neither group wanting to relinquish control. Eventually the government regained control, and Naandi operated its own bank for the farmers.

Partnership with government in perspective

Although AASSAV's commitment to working in partnership with the government continues, there have been both positive results and major snags: bureaucracy, corruption, general apathy and political ambitions have often been hindrances. Some examples are outlined here:

- *Late disbursement or no reimbursement of funds:*

Attitudes to money in India are complex; the fact that money has not been committed to a project is not seen as a hindrance. Government officials will discuss the implementation of programmes by AASSAV and suggest that work on a project might be started with the promise that the money will follow, without the actual disbursement of funds. But AASSAV discovered the hard way that promises made by government officials often come to nothing. When promises were taken at face value and were not fulfilled, AASSAV itself had to bear the costs. Thus they learned never to carry out work requested of them unless a contract had been signed and the first payment had been made. Challenging government officers to fulfil the promises made by them is a difficult task; work in other areas is likely to be hindered if confronted.

Payments are always difficult to obtain. At each stage a government officer has to come, check the work and give his report. While it is right that checks are made to ensure the work is properly carried out, even when all procedures have been followed local officers often delay payment and the final amount is usually, for one reason or another, withheld. The number of visits which have had to be made to the ITDA headquarters at Paderu – a round trip of 100kms – to obtain the payments means that costs for AASSAV rise and savings reduced. One argument often used was that AASSAV, because it was in receipt of foreign funds can easily pay for projects. But, like most NGOs, AASSAV survives on a tight budget with all of its income accounted for.

Even on the completion of a programme the government has been known to retract its promise of final payment. When a programme is left incomplete in this way, AASSAV loses its credibility with local people, a much more difficult situation for a local NGO which cannot escape than for a government official who can! Tribal people are reticent about asking for funding, but as programmes must be paid for, the management team has had to learn not to do anything until funding has been secured.

One example of this was the savings and credit scheme which was a collaborative project between AASSAV and DRDA. It had taken many months to get the funds for the construction work to start, and when the building work was near completion, the final payment was promised by the local Mandal office before the project director was moved on to his new position. Two days after this promise was made, it was withdrawn with the statement that there were no more funds available. The reason for this was not known and it can only be surmised that the project director had overspent. Whatever the reason,

AASSAV would have to foot the bill. Clearly, the conditions they have to work under make financial sustainability frustratingly difficult for AASSAV.

- *Keeping appointments*

AASSAV leaders have frequently visited project offices only to find that the person they need is not there, even when an appointment has been made. They often have to go as far as Visakapatnam (a journey of more than three hours) and have the frustration of finding that the officer has not turned up. "Come back tomorrow", the other staff say … and this can go on for days. Work on the project can be brought to a standstill when the workers can neither find the relevant official in his office nor persuade him to make a visit. It is only the top official who can finally issue an order, and so there is little point in discussions with others until agreement has been given.

- *Continuity*

Projects usually have to be implemented quickly, because the heads of the agencies are moved on at short notice. They are generally in their post for two years before they are transferred to another position. Each new officer has the power to initiate his own projects and will not necessarily continue a previous director's project and so the potential for long term development is limited through lack of continuity. *A long term strategy which allows for follow up would enhance the chances of projects becoming self-sustaining and successful.*

- *Monitoring and support*

Government staff shortages result in insufficient monitoring and follow-up of projects so that when difficulties in implementation are encountered by local communities, there will quite likely be no one available to help. Local NGOs such as AASSAV on the other hand can give invaluable assistance to government projects by supporting implementation and providing follow-up.

- *Corruption*

Finally, the corruption which occurs at all levels of government in India is a real hindrance to sustainable and consistent development reaching the neediest. It is a well-know fact that funds are often misused with only a small proportion of it applied to the actual work for which it was intended. It happens too that, if local leaders do not comply with the wishes of government officials, hindrances can be put in the way of development. Tribal people will often bow to such pressure and actions are sometimes taken by AASSAV officers which are difficult to account for in the Executive Committee, to the Board of Directors or to donor agencies. Everyone talks about this issue; everyone knows it goes on, yet no one seems to want to check it.

Despite these problems, AASSAV still attempts to maintain a good relationship with the government. Why should it take the trouble to do so? Because the vision needs to be embedded in government structures; implementation in government institutions needs to be ensured for the long term:

- government needs to be encouraged to budget funds regularly for development activities

- policy change is essential (although AASSAV's explicit purposes do not include advocacy, the activities and experiences of the organisation do in fact advocate for tribal development.)

- government officials need to understand the real development needs in the tribal communities.

It is said that until tribals themselves begin to fill these official government positions development will continue to be slow, but even then the conventional bureaucratic processes of government institutions are likely to continue to put obstacles in the way of progress.

Relationship with Donors

Fowler (2001) points out that practically all development work carried out by NGOs is "*influenced by the quality of donor assistance*" (168) and that unless the donor agency is included in the investigation of project effectiveness, learning about development initiatives will remain inadequate. Since it is the donors who usually demand investigations, their own processes and procedures are rarely included as an aspect of research. As a result NGOs are often blamed for the failure of development projects when donors should in reality bear some of the responsibility (ibid).

Quality and commitment in partner relationships are, therefore, an essential part of the development of any NGO:

> "*... much would change and give confidence to the [NGO] staff if the donors would be fully committed. ... donor agency staff*

have their secure salaries, but [NGO] staff are required, or
expected to perform above and beyond what donor agency staff
are ready to give NGOs and their projects." (Gustafsson,
Interview, 2002).

These comments were made in reference to repeated requests for
studies and modified proposals before funding would even be
considered. This is not an unusual situation: it is the donor who makes
the demands while the local NGO, the recipient, has to comply.

The following section examines the positive and negative aspects of
the donor partnerships with which AASSAV has had relations.

Literacy, Education and Development (LEAD)

LEAD, the development office of Gustafsson's home organisation in
Canada, were ultimately responsible for the finances given to
AASSAV. Gustafsson liaised with LEAD from the field and the
manager of the LEAD office visited AASSAV twice a year to deal
with the accounts. On the basis of these visits and Gustafsson's
reports, LEAD prepared the actual proposals which were sent to the
donor agencies. In retrospect it would have been wiser if there had
been more direct collaboration with AASSAV leaders in accounting,
reporting and in the making of proposals to increase the capacity of
AASSAV, and although this was attempted, as stated earlier, many of
those who had been trained left. Although Gustafsson was in the field
and his reports were discussed with the leaders of AASSAV, there
was little direct contact with LEAD.

Canadian International Development Agency (CIDA)

Prior to AASSAV's being established, the literacy programme had
received funding from CIDA from the late 1970s until 1987 for
production and printing of literacy books and for literacy classes. In
1987, CIDA's policy changed and funding for literacy alone would no
longer be offered. If the literacy management team wanted to
continue with funding, they had to move into development work.
CIDA suggested that income-generating projects would enable them
to become self-reliant and to fund their own literacy programmes. As
described earlier, it was in response to these new conditions that
AASSAV was formed.

Thus when AASSAV was first established in 1988, CIDA was its one
major funding agency, and although LEAD in reality was an equal
donor, CIDA was the dominant partner, sending evaluators and
requiring reports to assess the programme. While the evaluators made

recommendations and LEAD and AASSAV attempted to follow these recommendations, no other assistance, either in capacity building or in technical support was offered. This left LEAD and AASSAV alone to direct the work.

Attempts to become financially self-reliant took all their capacity to manage and by 1997 literacy, one of the original aims of the Society, had ceased to exist at all. For seven years there were no literacy programmes as funds were not available. After 18 years, AASSAV's financial stability had still not been achieved.

Those who later partnered with AASSAV argued that changes would need to occur in AASSAV's structure and organisation before it would ever achieve a balance in its income generating projects, but while the funds were coming in, the structure and purpose of AASSAV were not under question. In 2005 when funding finally come to an end, AASSAV had to consider its next course of action. Although the most strenuous efforts had been made throughout its history to root AASSAV in its tribal setting, it is still an NGO with external funding, "doing development activities" within the surrounding communities. If AASSAV's survival may well depend on restructuring - to become an organisation built on and in the community with accountability and support from within the community. The future of AASSAV, as with any NGO, is unsure, and the outcome of changes which are indeed critical is unknown. What is sure, however, is that what AASSAV has achieved over the years of its existence has been remarkable. Many lives have been changed, many others touched in one way or another.

Relationships with non-governmental organisations

Throughout their relationship with CIDA, it had been recommended that AASSAV develop their contact with other organisations locally, nationally and internationally and they would have done so, had there been any appropriate organisations to relate to. Some attempts had been made, but relationships and partnerships cannot be forced and the process was not only time consuming, but very difficult for an indigenous organisation like AASSAV with no highly educated staff. They were able to take on local partners but broader networking was hardly possible when they needed to spend time and energy developing their own staff in management roles so that the organisation could function well autonomously. They did not have people qualified to send on deputations to conferences, for training or to visit other organisations, but relied on the expatriate coordinator for wider links.

Besides this, some of AASSAV's experience with other organisations caused them to be hesitant about developing relationships with outsiders, but eventually they did develop new partnerships with Indian based NGOs. The following are examples of attempts to develop relationships and provide services to others, illustrating that, while some partnerships have been beneficial, the attitudes and practices of outsiders are not always positive or helpful.

The coordinator of a German funded organization in a neighbouring district requested AASSAV to provide training for a tribal group. AASSAV agreed as it was well able to cope. The organization promised to cover the costs but, even after a letter was written to request payment, nothing was ever given. Although the cost was not great, this behaviour did not encourage trust between AASSAV and outside groups. As AASSAV attempted to keep to its commitments, including its payment obligations, it caused some disappointment when others did not.

It was suggested that AASSAV would be an excellent place for those working in development to conduct their research and a place for government officials (e.g. the Indian Administrative Service – IAS Officers) to study; and so it would, but their first experiences of academic visitors made the Society cautious. A PhD student from Andhra University and another from Osmania University, Hyderabad requested access. This was granted and AASSAV provided them with material, but nothing was heard of them after this. There was no feedback of any sort and AASSAV had no idea of what was written; whether positive or negative. Accordingly, when the next group came to request permission for research, they were refused.

Several Indian agricultural extension workers were to teach composting to local farmers on a Dutch government funded programme. Meetings were held at AASSAV headquarters, land was made available for the work, food and drinks were provided and considerable AASSAV staff time went into it. AASSAV were told that they would be reimbursed but they received nothing. Reneging on promises by first world organisations is most unhelpful in a context where the local workers are being trained in the ethics of good business practices.

AASSAV was selected as a venue for the celebrations of the UNpromoted International Year of the Indigenous People. The Museum of Man, a Government of India enterprise in Bhopal, organised events all over India. A representative from the Museum came to AASSAV and stated that AASSAV had been selected to host the event for this region. They sat together and made out the budget. The representative promised that everything would be paid for and if there were any additional expenses (and there were many as AASSAV found out) these would all be paid. The Director of the Museum, a famous Indian Anthropologist, representatives from the Department of Anthropology, Andhra University and many others attended. In the end AASSAV received about 50% of the budget and nothing at all for the additional expenditure. The coordinator wrote a letter to the Director, but never heard anything from him again. Such an experience was disheartening to AASSAV leaders.

An invitation was received from a newly established NGO based in Visakhapatnam wanting to promote marketing for tribal goods. Their aim was to put on a big exhibition. AASSAV did not respond, first of all because they had nothing to market through them, and also because this organisation would want its share of the profits. They worked out that by the time they would have travelled to Visakhapatnam, paid for hotels and food, there would be nothing left! AASSAV was beginning to discern the relative value of business and development opportunities heeding the warning signs where there is little likelihood of any positive outcome.

Capacity building within an organisation means to work with, and pass on skills and knowledge to the people themselves so that they are able to take positions of authority within the organisation. Development means the same within the community – passing on skills and knowledge so that development becomes integrated into the life of the community. This was what AASSAV had attempted to achieve and why it was a process requiring determination and tenacity, a route few will venture to follow. Most development work achieves little because not enough time and effort is given to building capacity. As Gustafsson pointed out in relation to the composting training which had taken place at the AASSAV headquarters,

> *"Everyone thinks that his project is very important and that everyone else should implement it. But the result of this programme is that no one is doing this composting anywhere. People do not learn through giving them a little course in a meeting hall somewhere. Even a little practical experience is not*

enough. It has to ... become part of their routine. It has to be done in their own fields and supervised again and again until it is a natural activity for them". (Interview 2001)

While many of these experiences sound discouraging, there have also been some positive links.

- AASSAV had links with the Central Institute of Indian Languages (CIIL), Ministry of Culture and Education in Mysore, where the Adivasi Oriya-Telugu-English Dictionary was published.

- The Newsletter was checked and edited by the faculty of the Department of Telugu at Nagarjuna University. The relationships with individual professors and university departments have been excellent.

The next example was one which could have developed into a positive long term programme, but after changes in personnel, the positive beginning was not followed up and resulted in disappointment for AASSAV and the local communities.

ActionAid

The relationship with ActionAid began when a Project Officer in the Paderu Agency in 1995, who was very supportive of AASSAV, left the government and joined ActionAid. Through him ActionAid came to AASSAV in 1996 to discuss long-term involvement with funding for 15-20 years. AASSAV willingly complied with ActionAid's principles of participatory development, and a Memorandum of Understanding was signed in 1996. Staff members were trained in participatory rural appraisal (PRA) methods in 1998 and a one-year feasibility study of the Baski Panchayat in Araku Mandal was approved for funding by ActionAid. This community comprised interior villages which had had little attention from developers in the past. AASSAV had had literacy projects there for some years and so had a good relationship with them. The village leaders had visited the AASSAV Headquarters and often asked for help and so this seemed an ideal opportunity to help the very poorest. Seven hundred and seventy seven families were interviewed using a very comprehensive survey instrument and the results were to act as a baseline for interventions. The report of the feasibility study sounded positive for the future of the development of this particular community, but when the feasibility study was completed the ActionAid project leader who had been in charge was unable to visit any more for family reasons.

The next project leader refused to visit the region and asked AASSAV leaders and the coordinator to discuss the follow-up phase in a hotel in Visakhapatnam. She asked AASSAV to put a project proposal together for 18 months' duration and for 300,000 rupees ($8000). Several projects were identified after the survey had been conducted and AASSAV put forward a proposal, which included a community hall and a drinking water tank at the point of a spring. This would save time for the women when they filled their water pots. Very little can be done, however, with 300,000 rupees and even this modest proposal amounted to over 600,000 rupees. ActionAid insisted on many changes to the proposal and funds for some areas of the project were not allowed or were hidden. AASSAV have always insisted on keeping its finances completely open so they refused to comply with this. AASSAV then put in a second proposal for literacy and village libraries.

By this time, the old friend had left ActionAid to return to a new government assignment. For a long time AASSAV heard nothing, but when finally ActionAid delivered their verdict, it was to the effect that AASSAV's views and working methods in development were different from theirs so they wanted to discontinue their relationship. AASSAV's annual report for the year 2000 states

> "*ActionAid communicated to AASSAV that AASSAV's development methods with tribal farmers do not match theirs, and that therefore ActionAid cannot consider a continuation with AASSAV.*"

In the letter from Action Aid there was no other explanation and no indication of what those differences were.

Although AASSAV benefited from what they learned, it had cost them financially far more than ActionAid had given to do the feasibility studies. There was another more serious repercussion of this episode, however. When AASSAV wanted to do some more work in the same panchayat, the people had become very wary of development organisations. The survey had held out a promise of help, but when nothing happened the local communities felt let down and a cynical attitude towards AASSAV surfaced. They had become accustomed to outsiders visiting and talking of investment which never materialised, and AASSAV, a locally run organisation, staffed by their own tribal people, had now done the same thing to them. The repercussions were serious in terms of injury caused to relationships with local communities in that area and AASSAV had much to do to regain their credibility and good name among the people.

As often happens, the funding agency was attempting to implement its own values over and above an indigenous organisation. This also illustrates the common and more injurious problem of engaging local people and communities at the grassroots without any guarantee of intervention or support. The voracious information needs of large agencies, coupled with elaborate planning processes, in-depth surveys, interviews and even experiments may, in fact, lead to nothing. That input from local communities into project proposals is a requirement is in itself laudable and right; however, agencies must consider carefully how far they can go without, as evidenced here, damaging both local organisations and local attitudes to outside assistance and intervention. Beyond that, there is an ethical question of how far the powerful should take up the time, consume the energies and exploit the knowledge of the less powerful or powerless and yet leave them with no additional tools or strategies to break out of their powerlessness at the end of it. This was a typical instance either of a serious failure of imagination or of a conspicuous lack of will to act with proper consideration. Granted that donors must do their research before assigning funds, they need to take into account the impact of their demands and ensure that there is as little damage as possible through the raising of false expectations and they should certainly at least give fair re-imbursement to these impoverished communities for expenses incurred.

The next two examples have both been more positive, though the organisations are totally different from each other and work using completely different models of development.

CARE India

CARE India, in conjunction with CARE UK and funded by the European Union, developed a proposal entitled the Sustainable Tribal Empowerment Programme (STEP). The proposal had been five years in preparation and working closely with the ITDAs in four districts, CARE and the EU carefully screened selected local NGOs to deliver the project. Only those that already had support from an international funding agency were eligible and AASSAV was nominated and accepted as one of the implementing agencies.

There was little contact between CARE and AASSAV in the initial planning phase of the STEP programme. The collaboration had been between the EU, CARE and the Government of AP. It was only after the plans had been made and the programme launched that AASSAV became involved. With the EU as the donor, representing participating European countries, and the Indian government's involvement, the project was more like a government to government project, with CARE as an intermediary organisation and AASSAV, along with other NGOs, at the end of a long process of negotiation. The project was complex and ambitious and there were many delays to the start of the programme which caused AASSAV problems in maintaining the staff levels in readiness for the work.

When the project eventually began, an office was set up with a computer and staff were trained to run it. Teams from the local NGOs were trained by CARE to conduct a survey within a PRA framework, and to document and assess the assets, needs and priorities of each village community (similar to the process conducted by ActionAid above). The local community discussed their own development and, within certain limitations, CARE and the local NGO developed a plan with the local community. Two hundred village 'animators' were employed and trained by the CARE project and these animators trained and supported local community based organisations (CBOs - school committees, farmer's cooperatives, development committees), providing a link between the needs of the community and provision, such as access to clean water. The project followed a rights-based approach aimed at empowering communities to access their rightful government resources. CARE planned that by the end of a 5 - 7 year period the village-level CBOs involved should be able to take the responsibility for development themselves, having learned how to access the resources.

The partnership between CARE India and AASSAV worked well, with well-trained field staff and the project manager operating closely with AASSAV supervisors and local animators. Involvement in the CARE project has been a positive experience for AASSAV and evidence of the activities of the project itself, such as provision of water to villages, was soon apparent.

However, as with the other experiences AASSAV has had, losses have been incurred. The initial promise of the CARE leaders made to the coordinator was that the STEP would build capacity in the NGOs so that after withdrawal of the STEP the NGOs could continue the programme. There has been capacity building within the STEP, but nothing for the implementing NGO itself. Furthermore, the president of AASSAV has given at least 50% of his time for the STEP without remuneration. AASSAV does not have sufficient core funding to maintain this level of involvement and all the activities of AASSAV's employees, even the president, should be covered by project funding.

Naandi

Naandi was originally set up by four major corporate companies based in Hyderabad as a funding agency, but it soon increased its capacity to implement and oversee it own programmes.

The relationship with AASSAV began when a field officer of Naandi saw a summary of AASSAV's work written by the coordinator at the office of another local NGO.   He arrived unannounced to find a thriving project based on a coffee plantation.   The CEO of Naandi was interested in AASSAV because of its indigenous nature and because of the environmental features of the projects and approached them to find out whether there could be any collaboration. After much discussion, it was felt that Naandi could support the Family Coffee Farmers' Project.

Developing a working partnership between AASSAV and Naandi was arduous.   From the beginning there were many hurdles to overcome and the negotiations took a long time.   AASSAV and Naandi had to learn how to relate to one other, and changes had to be made on each side to accommodate the other's views and ways of working.   Naandi had an efficient, professional, highly skilled, corporate outlook, while AASSAV was a developing tribal organisation.   Naandi had never worked directly with tribal people or a tribal organisation before, and AASSAV had never worked with an Indian based corporate NGO. But both persevered and a mutually beneficial relationship was built. AASSAV learned to stand firm on its principles, while developing a constructive partnership with an outsider while Naandi had to learn that trust takes time to grow and that decisions may not be implemented immediately or in the same way as they would be in a corporate organisation.   AASSAV leadership needed to be convinced that changes were needed, and these would have to implemented in a way which was acceptable locally.   Naandi had to understand that change would not be easy, particularly for the president who had, for the previous 15 years, held almost all power in a centralised manner.

From AASSAV's perspective the relationship has had both positive and negative aspects.   For AASSAV delays and changes, particularly relating to funding, caused problems for the local organisation as they attempted to build trust and confidence with the local community. AASSAV had sought to persuade people to risk their own time and energy on new a enterprise, while Naandi appeared to be vacillating.

From Naandi's perspective, agreements on accounting and reporting, and on changes in management, were not fulfilled. This was partly due to the lack of ability within AASSAV to fulfil the demands: demands that were often, in fact, unrealistic. Naandi appeared to want to bypass AASSAV, spending little time building capacity, instead bringing people in from outside to manage the work. Without AASSAV, however, without the local knowledge and the understanding of the community that AASSAV brought, it would not have been possible for Naandi to operate effectively, if at all, in the tribal area. The language and cultural differences would have been too great.

Naandi argued that their goal was to build capacity, but that their commitment was not necessarily to AASSAV; it was to the tribal region and population as a whole. Naandi recognised that AASSAV had the scope to expand its base and to reach out to a wider population, to be a catalyst for the development of the region, but for AASSAV to be part of this greater vision, it would have to make some tough decisions. AASSAV needed to look at its limited resources, to use them to best advantage and to make itself more relevant to the local public. It would have to reduce its projects, at least those which were losing money, and channel its resources more appropriately. Naandi suggested that rather than a membership organisation AASSAV should be a representative of the people; an apex organisation supervising and assisting in local development projects.

Naandi is keen to demonstrate that development can be efficient as well as effective, but this can only be done in relationship with local communities, taking into consideration their perspectives and desires. For all the difficulties in developing trust between the organisations, the Coffee Farmers Project is functioning well, and farmers are already seeing the benefits. A Naandi office is located on AASSAV premises and a manager chosen by Naandi is in charge of the work. Former AASSAV staff who are experienced in coffee growing and in processing have become supervisors.

It took a long time to establish a working relationship with Naandi – one which continues to develop, but not in the way originally intended - and it was not just AASSAV which has had to change. Both AASSAV and Naandi would agree that they have learnt a tremendous amount by working together.

A chronology of partnership: Naandi and AASSAV

1998-2000	AASSAV was asked by the District Collector and the ITDA to manage the coffee planting programme. 1407 families were selected for this project but after 12-15 months of coffee planting, there were no funds for ongoing support for the farmers. Many did not have the ability to develop their new plantations.
2000	Visit to AASSAV by Naandi field staff
2000	The EC together with the Coordinator worked on a proposal for Naandi. Talks went on for over a year and at last an agreement was negotiated whereby Naandi would be partnering with CIDA in supporting AASSAV with the development of 1000 coffee growers and their families.
October 2001	The CEO of Dr Reddy's Laboratories, a multinational pharmaceutical company which is supporting Naandi, along with the CEO of Naandi, stayed at AASSAV headquarters and visited some interior sites. They were very positive and promised to support AASSAV as an organisation both in building its capacity in management and organisation and by assisting its work in the community. AASSAV had many needs, which had been recorded in reports and evaluation documents, particularly in the areas of finance and accountancy, and monitoring and evaluation. New projects meant that the need was all the more urgent. Naandi committed itself to supply many of these needs and to train the management side to bring AASSAV to a place where it is an efficiently run organisation.
November 2001	The first cheque was supposed to arrive one week before the first 2-day training period for 250 of the farmers would begin at the centre. The timing was crucial: the fertilizer had to be applied and protecting walls put in place before the dry season when animals are allowed to roam free and would destroy the young plants. But it didn't

	happen. Naandi decided they needed more information before they could release the funds. So support for the farmers was again delayed.
January 2002	The survey form was improved and eventually ready. The supervisors and area representatives conducted the survey over two or three weeks. The questionnaire was very comprehensive and because it took a long time to feed into the computer, the project's starting date was delayed once again.
11 March 2002	The proposal and budget were accepted and the agreement was signed. The project was formally started at AASSAV.
12 March 2002	The final draft of the budget was sent to Naandi by fax.
14 March 2002	The first batch of 250 farmers arrived at the AASSAV headquarters for the meeting, 6 months later than it was originally planned for.
15 March 2002	AASSAV was told that the budget was being rewritten and asked if they could use the CIDA funding for the moment.
Nov 2002	Programme Advisory Committee made up of AASSAV leaders, Naandi, and outside experts established to analyse and advise on ways to improve AASSAV's activities and performance.
April 2003	68 literacy centres once again established after a gap of 7 years.
	The AASSAV Executive Committee, after long deliberations, signed a resolution asking the Naandi Foundation to take on the responsibility for managing the MACS Bank. The Naandi team organized the election of the Board, preceded by many meetings with the SHG officers in interior

April 2003	areas. Naandi aimed to reorganize the management of the bank as the loans were not being repaid on time and the books were not balancing. Difficulties in gaining the necessary financial documentation from the bank for DFID support meant that funding was not granted. Naandi had to rethink their proposal, and look for alternatives to the MACS bank for their own savings and loans groups. Naandi's new proposal was not entirely acceptable to some local bodies, but to operate efficiently, the bank had to work without outside interference from government or NGOs. And monitoring of both bank staff and SHGs (Self-Help Groups) was essential in order for the bank to operate without loss.

There have been many difficulties between AASSAV and Naandi as AASSAV struggles to maintain its own identity while working with a large organisation: one of the main problems being the limited amount of time devoted to the development of solid working partnerships. Furthermore, there is an inherent imbalance in the relationship in that should funding run out or cease, or if there is a change in policy at the donor end it is the recipient organisation which will face the problem of sustainability, both of itself as an organisation and of its development activities.

Relationships with agencies in perspective

Behaviours and attitudes can either help or hinder the development of relationships between tribal people and those from outside. Outsiders are often critical of the apparent backwardness, giving the impression of superiority, implying that the solutions they provide are better than local solutions. It is refreshing when an outsider treats the tribal people with dignity and respect. Outsiders often lack the basic understanding of local circumstances and the subtle complexities of the social order that holds community and culture together. Time to understand the situation and build capacity appropriately is rarely given.

Most development agencies are based in cities and staff only come for short visits. Sometimes those in authority never visit the place at all. Even where there are people who understand and have worked at the grassroots, the lines of accountability with the larger agencies are so long that the consequences of actions seem at times to be ignored.

Many of the decision-makers are far removed from the operations and understand little of the results of their actions at the grassroots. Development has become a business. Tribal people have to answer to these organisations for what they do and the way they live in a way that city people are rarely questioned. City dwellers do not have to give an answer for their way of life, the way they spend their money, how they use resources, or dispose of waste. While government may recognise the inequities and the necessity for change, it is slow to reveal itself in practice at the grass roots.

Some development agencies are becoming more advocacy focused and less orientated towards providing actual services. AASSAV is action focused and doing the work is more important than direct advocacy; the medium is the message. AASSAV's advocacy role is one of demonstrating change within communities rather than lobbying for policy changes elsewhere which may have very little impact locally. These differences lead to difficulties with some potential partners.

In India relationships are important and have to be maintained to get things done. The idea that "one good turn deserves another" is significant, which means that are always such 'debts' pending. This puts pressure on the social life of individuals, and spills over into the organisation. Any service, work or funding provided, can be seen as personal involvement so that even when the money originates with a donor, it is as if an individual has given it, whereas in the view of most funding agencies, a service is independent of personal relationships. This can cause relational tension as for example, when the leader of the organisation that had previously helped to train AASSAV staff became ill. He expected the coordinator's help in paying his medical bills even though the work he had done was on a regular business footing and had been fully paid for.

There is always an area of intercultural mismatch – behaviours which are interpreted differently and whose meaning may escape one partner or the other. Time, sincerity and a learning attitude are essential in moving beyond the surface behaviour to its meaning.

CONCLUSIONS

The challenges for AASSAV have increased over the years as they have had to learn to work with a number of agencies with different agendas, expectations and demands. CIDA expected AASSAV to become self-reliant through income generation but the Indian government had a different view. From their perspective, AASSAV had gained a lot of experience and local knowledge which would assist the government in its development efforts and as a registered society it was helpful for government agencies to work directly with them. Naandi and CARE both expected AASSAV to serve the communities and so the main focus was outside of AASSAV.

There were many aspects of the organisation which need strengthening and new skills had to be acquired to manage a variety of projects with different, if related, focuses. In doing so, AASSAV had to learn to protect and defend the values, beliefs and ways of working they felt were important. In implementing projects, AASSAV staff gained experience of planning, supervising and monitoring, of recording correct data, and of financial accuracy.

The relationships that AASSAV has developed over the years, whether positive or otherwise, have all been regarded as part of a learning experience for the organisation, bringing it further into the national and international development world. There is now in AASSAV far reaching potential for the development of the region if appropriate structures can be found to correspond to the changing circumstances.

TOPICS FOR DISCUSSION

1.*'Participation is essentially a "learning by doing" exercise'.*
Why are partnerships between NGOs and other organizations
highly challenging enterprises?

2. How might local government facilities be made more 'user-
friendly' for tribal people?

3. Uwe Gustafsson's judgement after long experience is that
*'much would change and give confidence to the [NGO] staff if
the donors would be fully committed...'*. What arguments would
you adduce to convince a donor organisation to rethink its
policies in favour of full commitment? What counter-arguments
might the donors bring in response?

4. Everyone agrees that capacity-building is at the heart of
successful, sustainable development for any community. Why
then in practice is priority rarely given to this matter?

5. How can equality be achieved, in India, without a revolution?

CHAPTER 6

Sustaining Local Development

Vision and commitment are often taken for granted, though they are in fact fundamental to the sustainability of any action for socio-economic change. AASSAV's vision and commitment has sustained them through eighteen years of development for the Adivasi people of the tribal region. But financial stability, an essential component, has of all the goals proved to be the most difficult to achieve. There are also more pragmatic aspects to the sustainability of an organisation like AASSAV whose raison d'etre is the embodiment and expression of local commitment to change. There has to be a certain level of technical ability to maintain the projects, which has also proved difficult because of the number of well-trained employees who left. Then, the projects themselves need to be developed in such a way that lasting change occurs in terms of socio-economic development and positive environmental impact. This chapter assesses the likelihood and parameters of the sustainability of AASSAV as an organisation in the context of the development of the region as a whole.

Financial stability

CIDA first began funding in a substantial way in 1984 at which time only the literacy project was in progress. Beginning in 1987, AASSAV was established in order to move into income generation at CIDA's request. It was intended that AASSAV should be self-reliant under Adivasi leadership within that funding period of three years. Various income-generating projects were implemented in order that AASSAV might become self-reliant. Fowler (2001) observes, however, that NGOs are generally disappointed in this regard - the income they make is usually small in relation to time and effort and whether financial sustainability for development NGOs is ever likely is uncertain. Not unexpectedly therefore, or exceptionally, eighteen years later AASSAV still had not come to a place of financial security. It may have been more realistic to expect IGs to provide a limited amount of core funding, but to generate sufficient for projects as well is almost certainly unrealistic. Was it fair then to expect a local tribal NGO be self-financing when large international NGOs rely on fund-raising and donations to maintain their activities?

While such a goal is generally deemed unrealistic, some thought self-reliance should and could have been achieved. The reasons for the failure to become a self-sustaining organisation, therefore, are explained in the following sections.

External Funding

With funding from LEAD and CIDA various income-generating projects were implemented, infrastructure was developed (headquarter offices, chicken runs, sheep sheds), land was purchased, and administrative capacity was increased.

A problem for AASSAV arose when there were breaks in the funding. The first interruption happened in 1994 after AASSAV had received six years of CIDA funding. Everything seemed to be working well but then the application to CIDA was not submitted early enough and the closing date was missed. The next application could not be submitted for another 6 months and in the meantime the implementation of projects was delayed; some could not be continued.

The second gap was even more devastating. The funds for the 1997-2000 funding period had been approved by CIDA and were intended to set AASSAV up to become self-reliant by the end of this period. It was only then that AASSAV discovered they needed to obtain a Foreign Contributions Registration number from the Government of India without which funds could not be transferred. During the 18 months that it took to obtain the requisite document, projects suffered badly. The fodder crop was lost because of water shortage, cows lost their milk, and some died. The dairy farm was practically closed. Without the right feed, rabbits started to kill their young. Valuable staff members left during that time; at least 30 for better paid government jobs. They included some who had been trained in Chennai and Visakhapatnam, and some who had been specially trained to look after the projects' finances.

The funding eventually arrived during 1999-2000, but with this money merchants had to be paid, loans returned and staff given their due salary. There was nothing left over to start new projects. The negative effects of 18 months without funding were probably the biggest obstacle to self reliance, security and sustainability. While other factors undoubtedly contributed to AASSAV's inability to manage itself financially, (adverse weather conditions, adverse market forces, lack of technical expertise, insufficient knowledge of business operations) recovering from these gaps took a long time and indeed most of the original projects were permanently lost.

A new application was made in 2000, but CIDA rejected it. Since the difficulty had been caused not by AASSAV but by outside factors, an appeal was made that the application be re-considered. CIDA sent a project evaluator to reassess the potential for self-sufficiency. Her evaluation was positive: that with the implementation of certain recommendations, CIDA should consider funding for a further period. Professor Cairns' report of 2000 also stressed the need to continue with funding. A report on the implications of not receiving funds was also submitted. CIDA finally agreed to more funding, but at a lower level, which meant that two new projects AASSAV was intending to implement had to be cut. While this was going on another year passed without funding: a third funding gap.

Again in 2004, at the end of the next financial period, AASSAV had still not attained financial sustainability. They had not regained all the ground that had been lost during the 18 month gap. It had been especially difficult to recover from the administrative staffing levels and capacity, particularly in the accounts department where three well trained staff left. More staff had been hired, but it took time to train them. In the meantime, the projects with Naandi and CARE (India) had started, both in 2001. These organisations were locally based and it was expected that these would have a substantial input into the organisation and management of AASSAV.

A frequent problem for development organisations is the lack of long term financial security. Funding security is essential and NGOs must know they can rely on the donor's support.

> *"A precondition for effective development initiatives is that the resources needed during negotiation will be available over the long term. In other words, NGOs must be able to operate on the firm assumption that predicted incomes will be raised."* (Fowler 2001:131)

The problem of not receiving expected funding is rarely discussed. It is often dismissed as a minor problem, but NGOs rarely have sufficient funds to tide them over funding shortages and the results can be devastating. Delayed disbursements for NGOs are not uncommon and while the donor pays no penalty the consequences for the recipient are enormous (ibid:132). One of the main reasons given by donors for the delay in payments is that reporting of information by the NGO is behind schedule. But the insistence that payments can only follow reporting may be unduly legalistic, even cruelly harsh, in the *"real-life situation of resource-poor development environments"* (ibid, Note 12:273). A suggested measure to help deal with this kind of situation is that sufficient funds be put aside to cover at least two reporting deadlines.

There were other problems AASSAV experienced with regard to finances which weakened their ability to become financially sustainable. All the pre-funding work expected by partners and donors, such as surveys, information gathering, putting the requirements in place, *itself* requires funds. Getting a project up and running calls for large expenditure on the part of the local NGO. For example, AASSAV made two trips to Hyderabad to meet with Naandi, they spent vast amounts of staff time on the project proposal and made many telephone calls and other communications. All of this had to come out of AASSAV's own funds. These "peripherals" are expensive to the local NGO, but donors rarely take this into account.

There are, besides, numerous ongoing expenditures for AASSAV, which most donors do not know about, or if they know, do not consider them their problem. AASSAV has to meet these expenditures or else it could not exist – and no collaboration would be possible. It would help if there were a general agreement that donors put an overhead allowance in. The normal minimum in international funding is 10% of the total budget. AASSAV has met with fierce opposition from Indian donors for this budget item.

Even though AASSAV has experienced great difficulties, particularly during the periods when there was no funding, the tribal people remained committed to the Society and its aims. Although many did leave, for others, it is not just a job; AASSAV is something that belongs to them and that they believe in. They know that they will get results only with dedicated input. They have to maintain their commitment through good times and bad.

External funding has ceased for the time being, which may even prove to have a positive outcome. AASSAV required reorganisation and streamlining to match the changing development needs. The IGAs which were not producing income were closed down, some being sold off to members. For example the mill was sold, then established in the local village and run as a private enterprise. The new owners and the villagers were very willing to support this initiative: without it the villagers would have to go the 5 kilometres to the township for milling, which is time consuming and costly. The driver of the vegetable van applied to ITDA for his own van and now operates this business on his own rather than through AASSAV. Under private ownership both enterprises are making money.

Project Income

CIDA's evaluation in March 2001 stated that very few of AASSAV's income generating projects were breaking even, let alone making a profit. While the AASSAV team put this down mainly to the effects of the funding gaps, from which they had not yet recovered, CIDA's evaluator suggest that the problems were as much due to other factors. The criticisms levelled at AASSAV included:

- They had had no specific training in developing small businesses, no guidance in the choice of projects, no help developing realistic business plans, and no risk assessment.

- The projects were started without enough thought for the market. It was argued that AASSAV needed to look more carefully at local needs and markets and build on local resources. If products have to be shipped out to the cities, the distances make transportation costs high. On the other hand there is no point trying to market products locally that local people cannot afford to buy. A connected problem was that the projects may have been too small in scale to break into the various markets available.

- The weather conditions were hot and dry during 2000 and the coffee harvest was not very good. The price of coffee had also come down and in 2004 some coffee plants became diseased

- The level of technical expertise and access to the right kind of expertise in the Agency area was limited for the range of projects AASSAV was involved in. Besides this, it was difficult to get trainers to stay for more than a day - or a week at the most. Training had not been sufficient in agriculture or on the technical side.

- The number of staff was far above what was needed for the state of the projects, but no one was laid off. AASSAV's unwritten and unspoken policy is not to dismiss, not to sack, and not to retire anyone. That would be inappropriate in the culture, but this led to unsustainable staff costs.

- AASSAV had unrealistic expectations of success as, with the exception of coffee and black pepper, either the income generating projects were too small, or the costs of inputs too high, to allow them even to break even.

CIDA evaluators have argued that the projects could have been managed in a more business-like manner, particularly when it came to staffing levels. AASSAV counter-argued that this organisation cannot be treated entirely like a business and that there were valid reasons behind the decision to maintain an apparently high level of staffing. CIDA may have seen what looked like over-staffing but on closer inspection they will find that staff are not paid for time not worked. Tribal culture tends also to lead to 'unbusinesslike' levels of absenteeism. In this context it was quite an achievement when in 2001-2002 staffing levels began to be drastically reduced following the new administrator's advice and reorganisation. By 2004 staffing levels had dropped from 299 to 134 with reductions continuing.

By 2004, the majority of the projects had been terminated. Only those run by Naandi and CARE continued along with AASSAV's own coffee plantations.

There is sometimes a tendency to excuse AASSAV and attempts made to explain away the problems because of culture, or some other factor; but there have been problems, and these need to be acknowledged. The fact is that AASSAV operates in the real world and must learn how a local organisation can and should relate to economic realities and partner with other organisations of development. But AASSAV *has* shown its ability to adapt, indeed has had to adapt for its own survival. As the Society interacts with others, a balance, or even a compromise, is gradually being worked out through the tensions and problems – a balance between an organisation that continues to embody the development aspirations of a marginalised tribal group and to be run by them, and the wider world (increasingly globalised) in which not only the organisation but also the people now have to find their place.

Managerial stability

The coordinator was initially responsible for AASSAV's accounts while LEAD carried out audits to submit to its main donor, CIDA. LEAD also developed all the budgets and carried out the accounting based on figures received from AASSAV. As the funding base expanded and new donors were involved, members of AASSAV required more managerial and financial training to improve the planning and accounting systems.

Initially, the grants provided by CIDA had no stipulation on them except that income-generating projects were to be developed in order for AASSAV to become self-reliant and self-managing. Some may suggest that self reliance could have been achieved, even with the funding gaps, if the finances had been handled in a different way and the programmes had been planned with cost effective controls in place. Where there are no controls - and it was generally agreed that there were probably not enough in the past - money will be wasted. Waste can be avoided by ensuring the right conditions are in place prior to implementation and activities are followed up by proper evaluation, review and reporting. With this kind of financial discipline, particularly with regard to superfluous staffing, the investments made by LEAD and CIDA should have shown some benefits. But this view is purely a business view, and conditions other than financial have to be taken into account to understand the full nature of AASSAV's development as a self-reliant organisation. While we may not yet have seen the successful achievement of the full scope of AASSAV's hopes and dreams, the fact remains that through the ups and downs, the trials, disappointments and occasional triumphs, the tribal people are gathering valuable experience as they interact with and to some extent join the 'modern world'. They are in this way learning the skills with which they can gain their independence.

It is impressive how far tribal people have come in a few years: dealing by themselves with the planning and management of projects. Until very recently they were illiterate, marginalised and oppressed, unable to combat the inexorable pressure of the outside world on their traditional lifestyle. It will take time for the concepts associated with modern business methods to become firmly integrated into their mindsets, which have developed until now in relation to a self-sufficient rural economy in which they have been accustomed to live simply from one day to the next, and often from hand to mouth.

Environmental Sustainability

One of AASSAV's main achievements has been in its environmental impact through the transformation of waste land into plantations. Building on this Naandi, who also plan to withdraw at some stage, took on 1000 coffee farmer's plantations. This could not have achieved without AASSAV's initial intervention with support from the ITDA and without the tribal supervisors and facilitators who were trained by AASSAV.

Improved and Sustainable Environment

The Memorandum states in Section 4 that *"for the achievement of the*

CULTURAL AND SOCIAL OBJECTIVES the Society shall (vi) work for the improvement of the environment with particular emphasis on consciousness of the value of forests, and be actively involved in reforestation and Social Forestry".

In the matter of reclaiming land AASSAV have achieved much. Environmental sustainability can be done, it *has* been done - land has been reclaimed from waste to productivity. All of AASSAV's land was bought as waste and semi-waste land. The plantations that were once wasteland are now green places producing an abundance of high quality products, using entirely organic materials from the environment. AASSAV have done an excellent job proving that land, seemingly unsuitable for growing anything, can become green, pleasant and productive.

AASSAV have been heavily involved with projects designed to address both tribal poverty and environmental degradation at the same time. They have had model plantations and farms which show what can be done with marginal, waste or semi-waste land. More productive land provides an improved economic base to individual farmers and to communities. The transformation includes improved soil conditions, reversal of soil erosion and an environment in which fauna and flora flourish. AASSAV's commitment to good management of the environment has antecedents stretching back even before the birth of AASSAV: through previous literacy programmes a newsletter was distributed which gave prominence to articles on environmental issues and land improvement.

Within AASSAV all energy, land and water management has been carried out with environmental improvement in mind. AASSAV has electrified three of its plantations. Electricity is used for lighting, office work, print shop machinery and irrigation pumps to the extent that the supply is available. Kerosene lamps were used in the adult literacy centres. Two or three diesel engine jeeps are operated as well as a few diesel pumps for irrigation.

AASSAV land policy allows for marginal tribal land to be purchased from individual tribal farmers. This marginal land is by definition unproductive. It is unproductive because, since deforestation, the soil has been eroded and leached of nutrients and very little humus has been added since. Stone and rocks usually cover the surface. An individual tribal family will have done little to improve this marginal land, partly because of ignorance, partly because of lack of resources. The AASSAV committee purchases land from the tribal farmers above the advised government rate. As well as this, a promise is made to every family that AASSAV will enrol at least one family member as a member of AASSAV and provide employment for him or her on a full time basis on the plantation. The family is then cultivating its ancestral land and seeing it become productive for the first time, although it is now under AASSAV management. Restoring productivity to an area of wasteland is a careful, staged process: the land is terraced, stones are removed, a live fence planted with wild bush plants, compost and manure purchased and added to the soil and trees are planted. A composting programme has been set up on each plantation and all vegetable matter is being composted. The compost method was refined during 1994 and improvement in the condition of the soil has been noticeable on those plantations which have been in existence for some time. On AASSAV plantations over 40,000 trees have been cultivated, among them many fruit trees. Fodder, mulberry trees, coffee, bananas, and papayas are also being cultivated. Multi-layered cropping is practised. Organic certification was obtained by Naandi in 2004.

AASSAV has irrigated its lands with water pumped from rivers and several bore wells. Flood irrigation has been used where funds do not permit more efficient and effective irrigation. Through the CARE STEP tanks have been built channelling spring water for drinking and other purposes into several villages - an improvement which particularly benefits women.

Improved environmental management – the challenges

Energy, land and water management in the Agency Area as implemented by the government and practised by the tribal population has to improve and become more environmentally acceptable. The degradation of the environment is very closely related to the poverty of the people and present efforts, although positive in some aspects, have not stopped the destruction. In order to have a real impact action on a large scale is necessary. Improved environmental management requires the broad application of effective methods throughout the tribal area. This can only be achieved through the active participation of the tribal population in a programme of simultaneous environmental awareness raising, training in improved environmental applications and a continuous participatory monitoring, supervision and teaching programme. But a programme of environmental improvement will be effective only if it can be shown that it results in an improved lifestyle for the individual tribal family. Therefore it must be designed to run alongside a programme of economic improvement.

Traditionally firewood is still the predominant fuel for all households.

Electricity in villages is either non-existent or its supply is erratic. Villagers burn small kerosene lamps in their homes for lighting.

With the management of the land, the government soil conservation department is working on terracing projects with the tribal farmers and the government is encouraging and giving assistance to tribal farmers to plant social forestry plots on marginal land. The land is tilled with buffaloes, cows or bullocks and tribal farmers apply whatever manure collected from their animals onto the land. Smaller plots, or very steep fields, are worked by hand with a hoe.

The problem of a good water supply for both irrigation and drinking is a serious issue. The government irrigation department is assisting the farmers in small irrigation projects. Usually the method used is flood irrigation, but most fields are still rain fed.

Although government infrastructure and the implementation of certain programmes has improved, there has been very little fundamental environmental improvement. However, the tribal community should not only look to government programmes, but will have to realise their own responsibility in the process of both environmental and economic improvement. The Adivasis have an inherited understanding and knowledge of nature, an invaluable resource for the future sustainability of the local environment and, through being partners in their own development processes, they will be able to contribute to national and international development. The Farmers' Coffee Project is an example which gives real hope for the future in both environmental and economic benefits.

Conclusions: Reflections on Lessons Learned

Through the years, one criticism levelled at AASSAV has been that it was simply attempting to develop itself as an organisation that would make provision only for its members, rather than serving the wider community. It is the case that training courses, projects, businesses and other activities were conducted on AASSAV premises, by AASSAV staff. But the kind of pressure that came from donors and the kind of advice that they received meant that AASSAV had little leeway in the way it progressed. It is also worth bearing in mind that had there been no development of plantations and attempt at self financing, there would have been no model plantations, no nurseries, no expertise to help the future coffee farmers, no experience.

Lessons have been learned by AASSAV in the way it developed as a local organisation, but the attitudes of donors and other agencies to development have changed through the years. Much of this change is reflected in the approaches AASSAV has taken.

- They started with literacy only and moved to literacy and development.

- At first the NGO was a non-profit organisation and it moved to income generation to finance NGO activities. Now NGOs are becoming "business for profit" organisations.

- It was initially a channel for government and other donor agencies and then moved to IGAs for community improvement.

It is only with hindsight that the situation can be seen more clearly and statements of how things could have been done can be made. Some who have been involved in AASSAV from the beginning have suggested that the following lessons can be learned:

- The assumption that AASSAV should be an exclusively tribal organization still stands as being the right decision. Otherwise, the tribal people would only be 'workers' - subordinates not 'owners'.

- The Canadian office should have involved the tribal staff in decision-making regarding proposals and budgets. There should have been training conducted connected with this exercise.

- The Canadian office should have monitored the project more closely and had a clear system in place for flagging potential problems at an early stage.

- The Canadian office should have insisted that a professional business manager and finance manager be included in the proposal, and ensured that such persons would be installed at the time AASSAV began with income generating projects.

- With the introduction of a business manager and a finance manager, AASSAV staff should have had a proper pay scale with all the required government regulations.

- Under proper guidance of professionals, AASSAV's management team should have been trained along professional lines.

- The AASSAV leadership and members should have been involved in all phases of expansion to sustain a sense of ownership. This would then probably have helped in the taking of disciplinary actions against members, a sphere which had been left to the coordinator.

- AASSAV should not have discontinued the literacy programme.
The entire literacy and adult education programme should have
continued alongside the income generating projects and the
programmes planned for the tribal families.

- AASSAV should have made every effort to retain valuable staff.

- AASSAV should have had a Board of Directors from the
beginning. While this is easier said than done, with real effort,
selfless capable people, both tribal and non tribal could have
been approached for such development work of the tribals

- AASSAV should have decentralized power in the beginning. The
president's role should have been more strictly defined as one of
representing AASSAV. However, the reality is that when
AASSAV went through financial gaps it was the president who
kept the organization going.

It is all very well to make statements of what should have happened in
AASSAV's organisation, but the conditions under which AASSAV
operated were not easy or straightforward. There were funding crises,
loss of staff, lack of business acumen and adverse environmental
conditions. Development never happens in a straight line; there are
always achievements and successes while at the same time, setbacks
and obstacles.

The current definition of poverty is *"a human condition where people
are unable to achieve essential functions in life, which in turn is due to
their lack of access to and control over the commodities they require."*
(Fowler 2001:4) Development is a process that is intended to enable
people to gain control over their access to food, shelter, warmth,
health, education, and security; to confirm their sense of worth and
value, and to enable them to exert an influence over the decisions that
affect their lives. Development cannot be seen only in terms of
employment and economic improvement, but also in improved
services, access to education, and choices for individuals, families and
communities and must lead eventually to a better quality of life.

TOPICS FOR DISCUSSION

1. What if anything can be done to protect NGOs from financial insecurity?

2. You are part of a team aiming to initiate an income generating scheme in a tribal area. It is your task to draw up a business plan. What principles will guide your planning?

3. How far should the implementation of new ideas to improve the standard of living of poor communities be 'artificially' cushioned from harsh realities by intervention and subsidy from outside? Or should they rather learn to deal 'head on' with market forces, dismissive prejudice, unfavourable trading relationships and other facts of life?

4. How far does the successful example of AASSAV in bringing productivity to wasteland illustrate a general principle that outside intervention and organised teamwork are essential dimensions to the development process?

5. It is clear that environmental degradation is happening by default in rural areas such as the Araku Valley. What action should be taken to renew and restore the environment and by whom?

6. Why is 'development' necessary?

Epilogue

Another pleasantly breezy sunny day; it is March 2006 and women dressed in brightly coloured saris tied across on one shoulder, baskets on their heads and babies in slings at their sides, are walking briskly to or from the market. A jeep, full inside and out, people on the canvas roof and even on the bonnet somewhat obstructing the driver's view, is precariously weaving its way around the dangerous bends, swerving to avoid the larger potholes. Repairs to the monsoon damaged 10-kilometre stretch or road from Araku Valley to Hattaguda was supposed to have been carried out, but the funds were used elsewhere and the people of Hattaguda have more time to wait for a smooth journey into the township. As we turn a corner, a newly paved road is visible; one which reaches villages a further 10 kilometres into the hills.

Approaching the AASSAV compound things look much the same; the office buildings, the workshops and the guest house painted white and surrounded by a garden in which a variety of indigenous trees and flowers provide shade and colour as we drive in. The well-maintained coffee plantation can be seen behind the offices. I have already greeted the President and the Vice President on the road between Araku Valley and Hattaguda as they go about their work. People on the compound are busy pruning trees, a jeep drives in, a motorbike roars out, a car drives up and another visitor arrives. The coordinator, here for a visit of two months, is working on a report and warmly greets me as I walk into the office. Kantamma, a long-term member of AASSAV has made the guesthouse ready and food is soon brought in stainless steel containers. Walking round the compound I came across Kilo Pratap still hard at work with a group documenting tribal history, stories and culture. In another building, a group of boys are attending a residential school for dropouts run by the CARE STEP along with AASSAV. Next week, a literacy development workshop, supported by Tribal Welfare, NGOs and the local language communities will be held....

Reflecting on its 18-year history, memories are a mixture of joy and pain – of positive recollections and agonizing regrets.

The huge impact of the literacy programmes on a vast number of individuals, the experience gained through the various projects and the businesses, the environmental impact which AASSAV has had on the region one through the organic coffee plantations. Now, through Naandi, a farmers' organic coffee federation was established and is currently breaking into international markets through the Fair Trade Company – an incredibly positive result.

And now AASSAV is once again at a turning point; CIDA funding has ceased, and LEAD, the partner NGO in Canada no longer exists. There is no longer any outside funding to support the work of AASSAV. Starting and running new programmes is impossible and offering tenders for business opportunities is difficult. The only source of income is through the organic coffee, black pepper and projects which pay rent for using AASSAV premises. Many AASSAV staff have been paid their investment funds and laid off; most of the few remaining are either seconded to the Coffee Project or are employed in CARE STEP. As in AASSAV's previous experience, funds provided rarely cover the real costs and AASSAV continues to put time and effort, and whatever funds are available into on-going projects to ensure their success. AASSAV, still the only fully tribal organisation in this agency area, fails to benefit either in specific training for capacity building or financially from either government projects or partnerships with the larger organisations. Injustices remain and a tribal organisation such as AASSAV, which should by rights be encouraged and supported to operate in its own locality, rather than sidelined in the process continues to lose out to larger organisations who regard themselves as more efficient.

While there may be circumstances which are difficult for outsiders to handle, trust takes time to develop and long term commitment is necessary before equal partnerships can evolve. It is sometimes an offence to the local community that large NGOs maintain expensive offices in cities, paying big salaries to its employees, while ignoring the need to maintain the core administrative and operating costs of a small indigenous NGO in a remote tribal village. Local knowledge and expertise is not taken seriously by outsiders (particularly seen in the discrepancies in salaries) and the more powerful in the "partnership" hurt those who have to face this daily. Reaction is almost inevitable.

And questions remain: Why was it that officials from ITDA came to see the vermi-culture work at the Dairy Farm, which produced 26,000 kgs of bio-fertilizer last year, but failed to include AASSAV in implementing the project for farmers? Why do the government and other organisations fail to make use of AASSAV's vast experience and their ability to reach the tribal communities?

Why are AASSAV women's groups not given contracts for school uniforms? Why is it that the print shop remains silent while government printing contracts are given to companies in the plains? AASSAV is still unable to compete with cheaper goods and services, having yet to develop greater capacity to operate in the world of business. Where in the process are those who were once the focus of "development"? The high cost of development in remote areas needs to continue if there is to be a change.

While neither government agencies, nor outside NGOs could have established certain projects in this region if AASSAV had not already established a presence and gained experience, the role of the local organisation is ignored by these agencies. As one young man commented, although they do not like the attitude of outsiders towards their organisation or towards the tribals in general, it is hard for a small organisation like AASSAV to resist the patriarchal, superior attitudes which permeate non-tribal minds and organisations. AASSAV continues to need an advocate who will champion their cause, a professional manager who has the ability to preserve the dignity of tribal people and reverse the injustices of the current circumstances.

But the people remain optimistic; AASSAV has been through such times before. There have been gaps in the funding and they continued to operate with what they had as far as they were able. The President suggests that they will continue to look for funds, but in the meantime, they will continue with the programmes they have. Any income generated for the current activities go first to maintaining the organisation including vehicle maintenance and administrative costs. What is left is shared equally among the remaining members.

One effect of development in the area is that many more young people are now educated, but without employment. Some of the older tribal community members regret the fact that young people no longer want to work in the fields, or on coffee plantations, but instead have become lazy and have become a nuisance without purpose or ambition. The boys go to school and sit the exams, but their grades are weak. Teachers are not as good as in the cities and often there are no teachers for some subjects. Maybe the wrong kind of education is being provided. Education is seen purely in terms of academic study, but what is required is a land-based education. A school based on environmental concerns and on traditional and new agricultural methods would be more suitable and enable the students to develop skills and understanding of appropriate land-based activities. Agricultural colleges should be given a status equal to academic institutions. Strong leadership among the tribal people is required to gather this wasted energy and give it a more secure place in society.

As I walk in the evening light towards the village of Hattaguda, the sun retreats quickly behind the hills casting long shadows over fields of healthy vegetables. I pass the busy, now prosperous mill which was purchased from AASSAV a year ago, avoiding the cows and buffalo as they return home from grazing. I pass the newly constructed water tank where the women are washing their pots and collecting water, returning home with at least two full stainless steel pots on their heads. Smoke rises once again from the roofs of the houses making ready for the evening meal. The tribal people continue their struggle to improve their lives – and things are slowly improving. They know now that they will become the equal of others and second to none, even if the road to achieve this is still a long one.

REFERENCES

Chambers, R. 1983 *Rural Development: Putting the Last First* Longman Scientific & Technical, Harlow, and John Wiley & Sons Inc. New York

Collier, V. P. 1987 *Age and rate of acquisition of second language for academic purposes* TESOL Quarterly 21:617-641.

Cox, A. and Healey, J. 1998 Promises to the Poor: the Record of European Development Agencies *Poverty Briefings* 1: November 1998 ODI

Cummins, J. 1979 Cognitive/academic language proficiency, linguistic interdependence, the optimum age question and some other matters. *Working Papers on Bilingualism* 19:121-129.

Cummins, J. 1979 Linguistic Interdependence and the Educational Development of Bilingual Children, *Review of Educational Research* 49(2) Spring 1979:222-251

Cummins, J. 1981 Age on arrival and immigrant second language learning in Canada: A reassessment. *Applied Linguistics* 2:132-149.

Davis, Patricia M. 2004 *Reading is for Knowing. Literacy acquisition,retention, and usage among the Machiguenga.* SIL International, Dallas, Texas

Dutcher, N. with Tucker, G.R. 1996 *The Use of First and Second Languages in Education: A Review of Educational Experience,* Washington D.C., World Bank, Country Department III

Fowler, A. 1997 *Striking a Balance: A Guide to Enhancing the Effectiveness of Non-Governmental Organizations in International Development* Earthscan Publications Ltd., London

Gustafsson, U. 1991 *Can Literacy lead to Development? A case study in literacy, adult education, and economic development in India* Summer Institute of Linguistics and the University of Texas at Arlington. Summer Institute of Linguistics, Dallas, USA.

Marr, A. March 1999 The Poor and their Money: what have we learned? *Poverty Briefings 4*: ODI

Mehrotra, S. 1998 Education for All: Policy Lessons from High-Achieving Countries: *UNICEF Staff Working Papers*, New York, UNICEF

Matshazi, M. Mother tongue literacy: Importance of learning to read and write in one's mother tongue. *International Journal of Adult Education.* Vol. XX, 1987 3-4:50-53.

Rogers, A. 2000 Literacy comes second: working with groups in developing societies *Development in Practice* 10(2):236-240

Rogers, A. with Md Aftab Uddin (undated) *Adult learning and literacy learning for livelihoods* http://www.uea.ac.uk/care/Recent_Writing/COLLIT4.pdf

Turton, A. 2000 Sustainable Livelihoods and Project Design in India *Working Paper 127* ODI, London

UNESCO. 2002 Education in a Multilingual World, *Position Paper,* UNESCO Paris

UNESCO, 2005 Mother Tongue Based Teaching and Education for Girls, *Advocacy Brief* UNESCO Bangkok

Wagner, D. 1993 *Literacy, Culture and Development: Becoming Literate in Morocco* Cambridge University Press: Cambridge